A QUICK COURSE IN
WORD
For Windows

STEVE LAMBERT

JOYCE COX

PUBLISHED BY
Online Press Incorporated
14320 NE 21st Street, Suite 18
Bellevue, WA 98007   (800) 854-3344

Copyright © 1992 by Online Press Inc.

All rights reserved. No part of the contents of this book may be reproduced or transmitted in any form or by any means without the written permission of the publisher.

Publisher's Cataloging in Publication
(prepared by Quality Books Inc.)

Lambert, Steve, 1945–
   A quick course in Word for Windows / Steve Lambert, Joyce Cox.
   p. cm.
   Includes index.
   ISBN 1-879399-05-9

   1. Microsoft Windows (Computer programs) .   I. Cox, Joyce, 1946–   II. Title.

QA76.76.W56   005.4'3
                                         91-62152
                                         CIP

Printed and bound in the United States of America

   3 4 5 6 7 8 9 H L Z L 3 2 1 0

Quick Course® is a registered trademark of Online Press Inc. Windows™ is a trademark and Microsoft® and MS-DOS® are registered trademarks of Microsoft Corporation. All other products mentioned in this book are trademarks of their respective owners.

Contents

Introduction   iv

1 Word Basics: Writing a Press Release   1

An overview of creating, navigating, saving, and retrieving documents. While writing a simple press release, we show how to give instructions and apply a few simple formats.

2 Letter-Perfect Documents: Producing a Company Backgrounder   28

We produce a company backgrounder while covering outlines, the glossary, search/replace, spell-check, and grammar-check.

3 Eye-Catching Documents: Creating a Flyer   54

Word for Windows offers extensive formatting capabilities and almost limitless layout possibilities. Here, we discuss character and paragraph formats and then take a look at Word's styles.

4 Graphic Impact: Graphics, Tables, Charts, and Spreadsheets   80

In this chapter, we dress up a document by importing a graphic, creating a table and chart, and importing a spreadsheet file.

5 Reusable Documents: Creating a Letterhead   100

After generating a simple letterhead, we convert it into a template that can be used repeatedly. Then we show how to create and format headers and footers for multi-page documents.

6 More Reusable Documents: Using Word's Templates   116

We demonstrate a couple of Word's templates and then briefly explain how to modify their appearance and function.

7 Print Merge: Creating Form Documents and Labels   132

We show how easy it is to prepare documents for print-merging and also explore Word's versatile template for mailing labels.

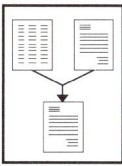

Index   149

Introduction

This book is designed to give you a quick-start in using Word for Windows version 2. Like all the books in the Quick Course series, this book introduces the basic concepts and techniques and makes it possible for you to produce documents you'll probably use often in your business.

We start in Chapter 1 by writing a simple press release and then show you how to manipulate Word documents in various ways. In Chapter 2, we develop a company information sheet (a backgrounder), and in Chapter 3 we combine the press release and the backgrounder to create a flyer. (The formatting demonstrated for the flyer could just as easily be used for a newsletter.) Gradually, you build experience with basic procedures and progress to more advanced techniques. You should read these first three chapters in sequence, being careful to save your documents when we tell you to so that you have what you need for future tasks.

You can read the last four chapters in any order, because each chapter focuses on a different topic and uses independent documents. In Chapter 4, we explore graphics, tables, and charts. In Chapter 5, we introduce templates and design a letterhead. In Chapter 6, we explore a couple of the templates shipped with Word for Windows and take a look at a macro. And in Chapter 7, we explain how to create form letters and other print-merge documents.

Word for Windows takes the labor out of producing your documents so that you can focus on being creative. It's exciting stuff. But, as you'll see as you work your way through this book, the real power of Word for Windows extends far beyond these familiar tasks. The release of version 2 may very well mark the turning point in the quality of computer software. Not only is Word for Windows a powerful, versatile, and relatively easy-to-use word-processing program, but it has been designed to allow you, the user, to modify its appearance and functionality to match your needs. You might think of Word for Windows version 2 as a Swiss army knife that comes with interchangeable blades and a kit that allows you to create any necessary new blades. You might customize your knife by adding a collapsible pen or a tape measure, while the guy down the street might customize his by adding a Captain Zork Cosmic Decoder module to his knife. Same basic knife, new purpose. How to customize Word is beyond the scope of this book, but we do give you a taste of what's possible.

Thumb quickly through this book now to get an idea of how things are laid out. You'll notice that we supplement our instructions and discussions with handy tips and other bits of information that aren't critical to the topic at hand but that you might find interesting or helpful as you learn the program. At the beginning of each chapter, we show some of the screens you will be working with and, as a memory jogger, we indicate the pages on which you will find information that you might want to look up later. Within each chapter, arrows draw your attention to features you might find yourself using again and again so that they are easy to spot as you quickly glance through the book.

Enough said. Turn to Chapter 1, and let's get started.

1

Word Basics: Writing a Press Release

Getting Started   2
Moving Around   4
Selecting Text   5
Giving Word Instructions   7
   Using the Toolbar, Ribbon, and Ruler   7
      The Toolbar   7
      The Ribbon   7
      The Ruler   12
   Using the Menu Commands   12
   Using Keyboard Shortcuts   15
Saving Documents   16
Retrieving Existing Documents   18
Creating New Documents   19
Manipulating Windows   20
Closing Documents   22
Printing Documents   22
   Setting Up for Printing   23
   Previewing Documents   24
   Straightforward Printing   24
Getting Help   25
   Looking at the Status Bar   25
   Using the Help Program   26
Quitting Word   27

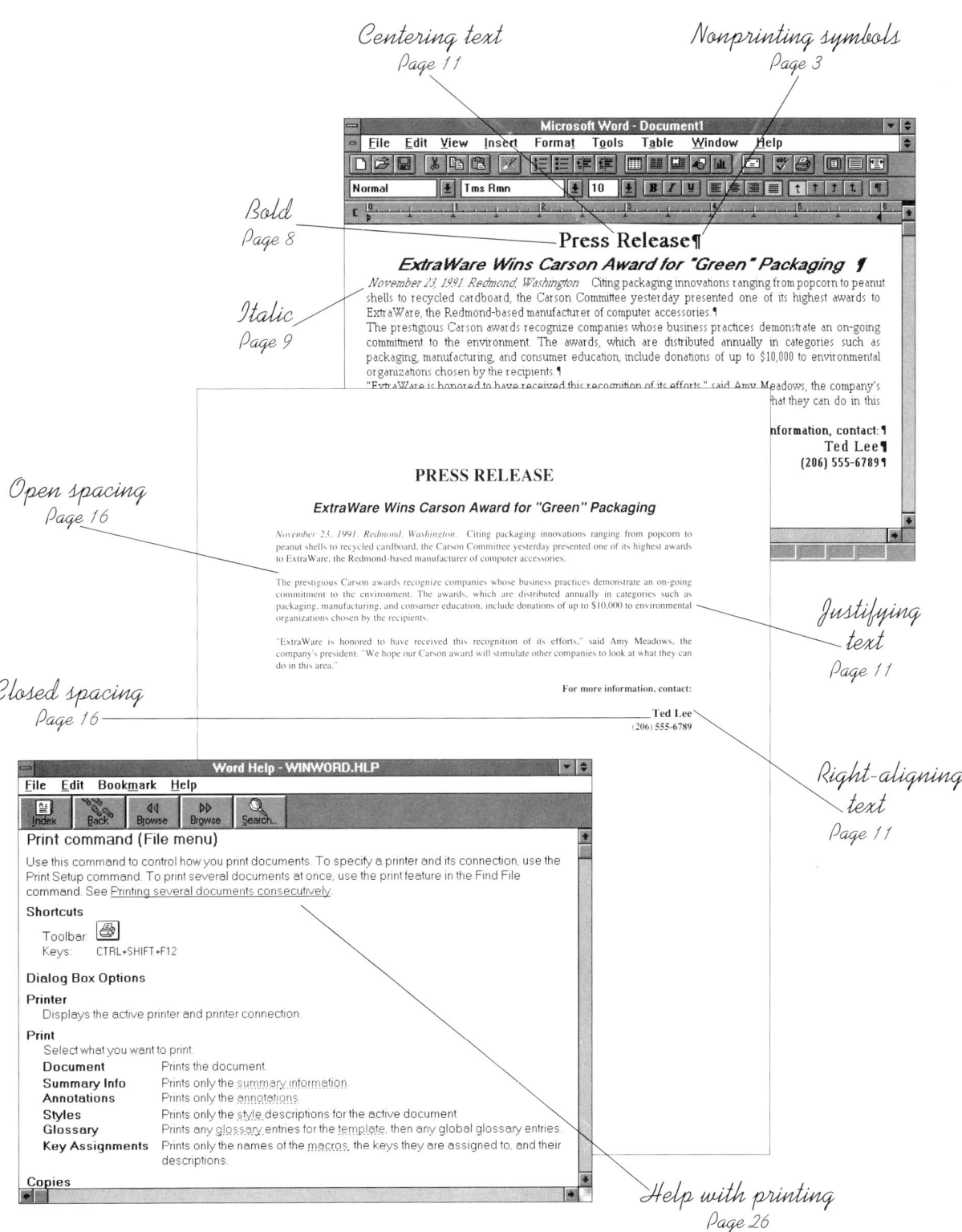

Most books about software programs have a chapter like this one. We tried to think of a way around it, but the fact is that if you have never used a particular program before, you have to get a few basics under your belt before you can do any meaningful work. You have to know how to save and retrieve files, how to enter text and move around a document with reasonable efficiency, and how to select text so that you can do something with it.

In this chapter, we cover all these topics while creating a short press release and viewing one of the documents that comes with Word for Windows. Along the way, we discuss basic formatting techniques, so by the time you finish this chapter, you'll know enough to create simple documents using Word. If you have used other applications that run under Windows, you might be able to get by with quickly scanning this chapter for Word-specific techniques.

Getting Started

We assume that you've already installed both Windows and Word for Windows on your computer, and that you're ready to go. (We don't give detailed instructions for installing the program because the process is so easy. Insert the Setup disk (Disk 1) in your A drive, type *win a:\setup*, and press Enter. Word will then guide you through the installation process.)

We also assume that you're using a mouse. You can work with Word for Windows using only the keyboard, but using a mouse with Word for Windows is, for the most part, more efficient.

If you have not already started Word, do so now:

Starting Word

1. Either type *win winword* at the DOS prompt, or double-click the Microsoft Word icon in the Windows Program Manager. (By default, the icon appears in the Word for Windows 2.0 group window.)

When Word is loaded, you see a blank window titled Document1, like the one at the top of the next page. We'll discuss each of the labeled elements as we use them in this chapter. (If the Toolbar, Ribbon, and Ruler are not visible in your document window, display them by choosing the Toolbar, Ribbon, and Ruler commands from the View menu; see page 12 if you need help choosing commands from menus. If the

Chapter 1   Word Basics: Writing a Press Release

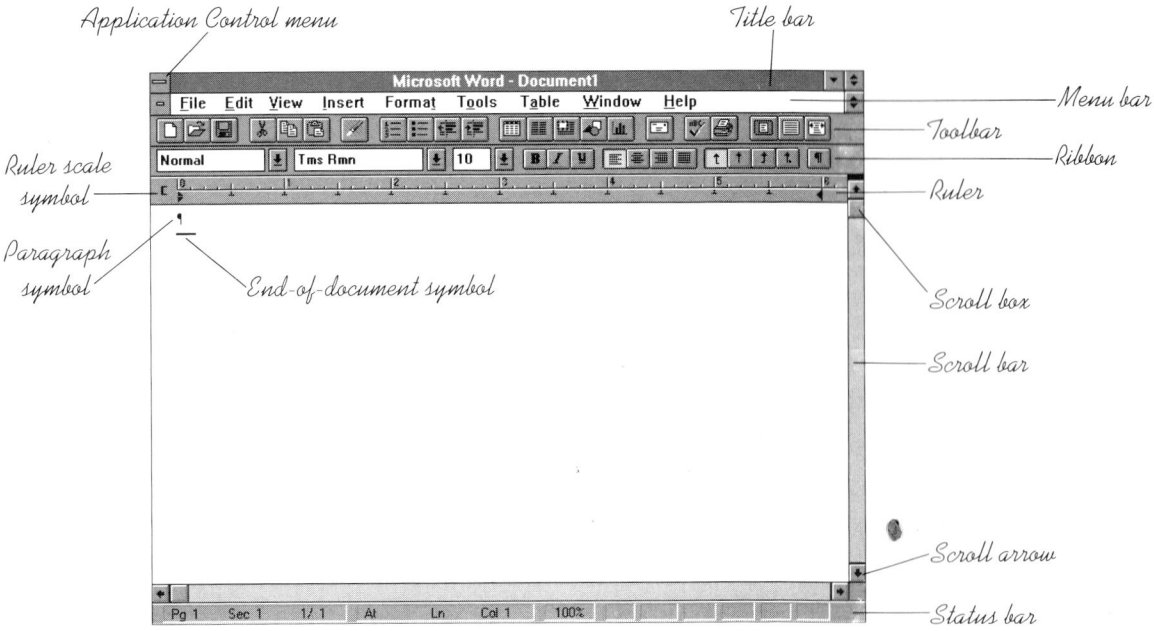

Word window doesn't fill your screen, click the Maximize button in the top-right corner of the screen.)

Maximizing the screen

Let's start by writing a press release. (You can follow along with our example or create a document of your own.)

1. The blinking insertion point indicates where the next character you type will appear on the screen. Go ahead and type the press release shown here:

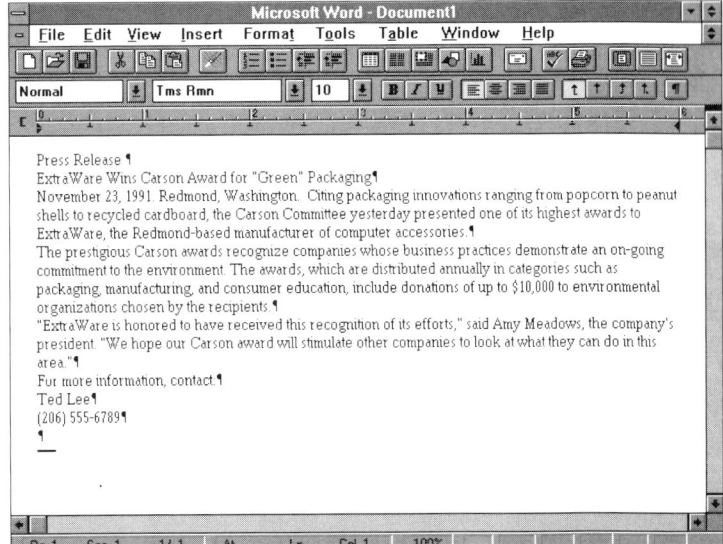

The ¶ symbols in the graphic are nonprinting symbols that indicate where we pressed Enter to start a new paragraph. If your screen does not display these symbols, click the ¶ button

Nonprinting symbols

at the right end of the Ribbon to turn them on. Don't worry if the lines on your screen break in different places from ours. These breaks are a function of your printer and the fonts you have available.

Now that we have some text on the screen, let's see what we can do with it.

Moving Around

You need to know how to move around a document for two reasons: so that you can edit the text and, if the document won't fit on the screen, so that you can view its contents.

When it comes to editing, the insertion point is where the action is. Clicking anywhere in the text on your screen moves the insertion point to that location, or you can move the insertion point with the navigation keys, like this:

Navigation keys

To move the insertion point...	Press...
One character left or right	Left or Right Arrow
Up or down one line	Up or Down Arrow
Up or down one screenful	PageUp or PageDown
To first character on screen	Ctrl-PageUp
To last character on screen	Ctrl-PageDown
To left end of current line	Home
To right end of current line	End
To first character in document	Ctrl-Home
To last character in document	Ctrl-End

Wordwrap

When entering text, press Enter only at the ends of paragraphs, not at the ends of lines. As the text reaches the screen's right edge, the next word typed automatically "wraps" to a new line (hence the term *wordwrap*). Pressing Enter ends the current paragraph and moves the insertion point to the beginning of the next line, ready to start a new paragraph. ♦

Clicking and double-clicking

To click something, move the mouse pointer over it, and then press and release a mouse button. (Unless told otherwise, use the left button.) To double-click something, move the mouse pointer over it, and then click twice rapidly. How fast you have to double-click is controlled by a setting in the Mouse section of the Windows Control Panel. ♦

Key convention

In this book, we indicate that two or more keys are to be pressed together by separating the key names with a hyphen. For example, *press Ctrl-Home* means hold down the Ctrl key while simultaneously pressing the Home key. ♦

Selecting Text

Before we do anything fancy with this short document, let's discuss how to select blocks of text. Knowing how to select text efficiently saves time, because you can then format the selected text as a group, instead of a letter or word at a time.

The simplest way to learn how to select text is to actually do it, so follow these steps to use the mouse to select text blocks of different shapes and sizes:

1. Point to any word in the document, and double-click to select the word and the following space.
2. Move the mouse pointer toward the left side of the window. When the pointer changes from an I-beam to a right-pointing arrow, it is in an area called the selection bar.
3. Position the arrow pointer in the selection bar adjacent to the line that begins *November*, and click the left mouse button once. Here's the result:

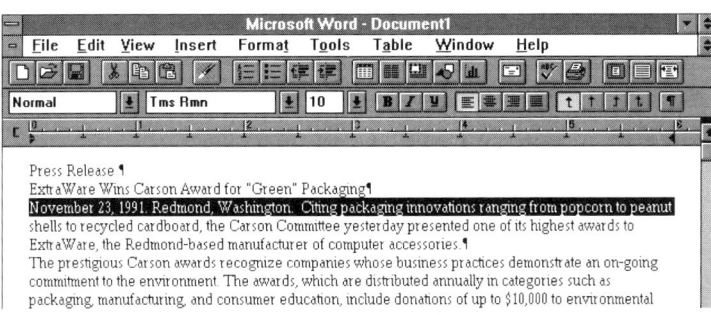

Selection bar

Selecting a line

Dragging to select text	Scrolling with the mouse	Invisible scroll bars
To use the mouse to select a block of text, position the insertion point just to the left of the first character you want to select, press the left mouse button down, move the mouse to just past the last character you want to select, and release the mouse button. As you drag, a highlight follows the insertion point. ♦	To view parts of a document that are out of sight without moving the insertion point, use the mouse to manipulate the scroll bars the same way you would in any Windows application. For example, drag the scroll box to the middle of the scroll bar to view information in the middle of the document, and then press Shift-F5 to return to the insertion point. ♦	If your screen seems to be missing one or both of the scroll bars, you can restore them by choosing Options from the Tools menu, highlighting the View icon, and then selecting the Horizontal Scroll Bar or Vertical Scroll Bar options. ♦

Selecting a paragraph

4. To highlight the entire paragraph, double-click in the selection bar next to the paragraph.
5. Move the pointer to the end of the next paragraph, hold down the Shift key, and click the mouse button. Word retains the existing selection and extends it to the position of the pointer.

Selecting the entire document

6. Move the pointer to the selection bar, hold down the Ctrl key, and click the left button to select the entire document.

You can also drag the pointer in the selection bar to select multiple lines or paragraphs. And you can drag through the text itself to highlight exactly as much or as little as you need.

Now let's select some text with the keyboard:

1. Press Ctrl-Home to move the insertion point to the first character in the document.

Turning on Extend-Selection

2. Press the F8 key to turn on Extend-Selection mode. The letters *EXT* appear in the status bar at the bottom of your screen.
3. Press F8 again to select the word next to the insertion point. Word highlights *Press* and the space following it, like this:

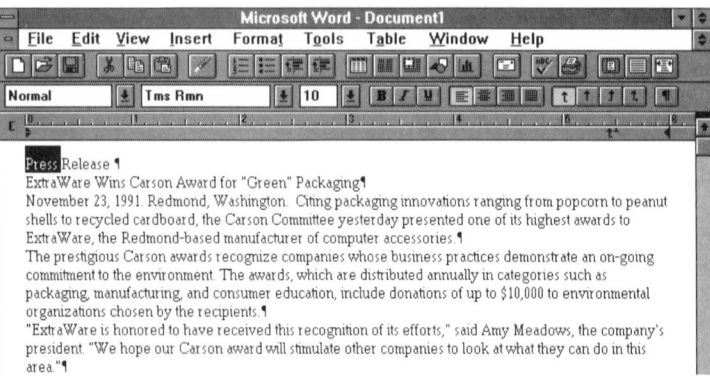

4. Press F8 yet again to select the sentence containing the insertion point. Now the entire *Press Release* title is highlighted.
5. Press F8 a fourth time to highlight the paragraph symbol at the end of the title, and a fifth time to highlight the whole document.
6. Now hold down the Shift key, and repeatedly press F8, shrinking the highlight until only the insertion point remains. Release the Shift key.

7. Next, try pressing different Arrow keys. As long as you are in Extend-Selection mode, Word extends the highlight in the direction of the key's arrow.
8. Press Esc to turn off Extend-Selection mode.

Giving Word Instructions

Now that you know how to select text, let's quickly cover how you tell Word what to do with the selection. You can do this in three ways: using buttons and lists on the Toolbar, Ribbon, and Ruler; using menu commands; and using keyboard shortcuts.

Using the Toolbar, Ribbon, and Ruler

The Toolbar, Ribbon, and Ruler all provide point-and-click ways of carrying out common word-processing tasks. Let's look at each of them in turn.

The Toolbar The Toolbar sports 22 buttons that access the commands and utilities you will use most often as you work with Word for Windows. We won't go into a lot of detail about these buttons now, but by the time you finish this book, you will have used most of them. For now, here's a visual tour of the buttons:

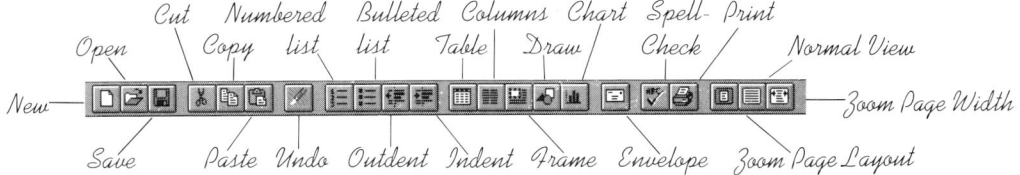

The Ribbon You use the Ribbon to apply common character and paragraph formats to a text selection. Character formats affect the appearance of individual characters. They can be applied to any number of characters, from one to the whole document. Paragraph formats change characteristics such as alignment, indentation, and tab settings for entire paragraphs. You can also apply character and paragraph formats by choosing the Character and Paragraph commands from the Format menu, but clicking buttons and selecting options from the list boxes on the Ribbon is much quicker.

The ¶ button at the right end of the Ribbon does not apply a format. As we've already mentioned, it simply turns non-printing symbols, such as tab markers and paragraph symbols, on and off.

Let's see the effects produced by some of the buttons on the Ribbon:

1. Move the mouse pointer into the selection bar adjacent to *Press Release*, and click the mouse button to select the heading.

Changing size

2. Let's increase the size of the selected heading. Click the arrow adjacent to the Size box (the third downward-pointing arrow from the left) to display a list of available sizes, and then click 18. The setting in the Size box changes to reflect the selected text's new size.

Bold

3. To set off the heading even more, click the Bold button on the Ribbon, and then click anywhere within the heading to remove the highlighting. As you can see, these two simple changes have a dramatic effect:

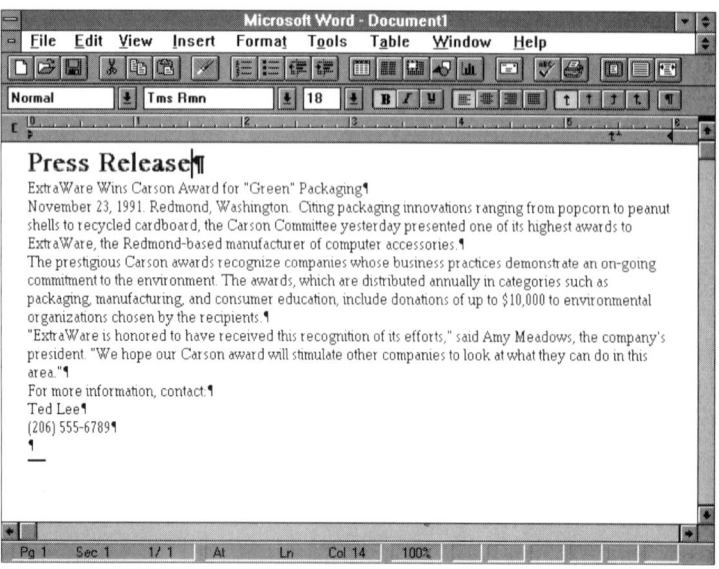

Notice that the Bold button is now lighter and appears to be "pressed," indicating that you have turned it on for the selected text.

4. Select the next line by clicking in the selection bar adjacent to the word *ExtraWare*.

Changing font

5. Let's change this heading's font. Click the arrow adjacent to the Font box (the second downward-pointing

Chapter 1   Word Basics: Writing a Press Release   9

arrow from the left on the Ribbon) to display a list of available fonts. Click Helv (or Helvetica). If necessary, use the scroll bar to the right of the list box to bring the font name into view. The setting in the Font box changes to reflect the new font.

6. Click the Size-box arrow, and select 14 from the drop-down list box.
7. Click the Bold and then the Italic buttons on the Ribbon.

Italic

8. Click an insertion point in front of November, hold down the Ctrl and Shift keys, and press the Right Arrow key until November 23, 1991. Redmond, Washington. is selected. (Include the period in the selection.)
9. Click the Italic button, and then click a blank area of your screen so that you can admire the work you've completed so far:

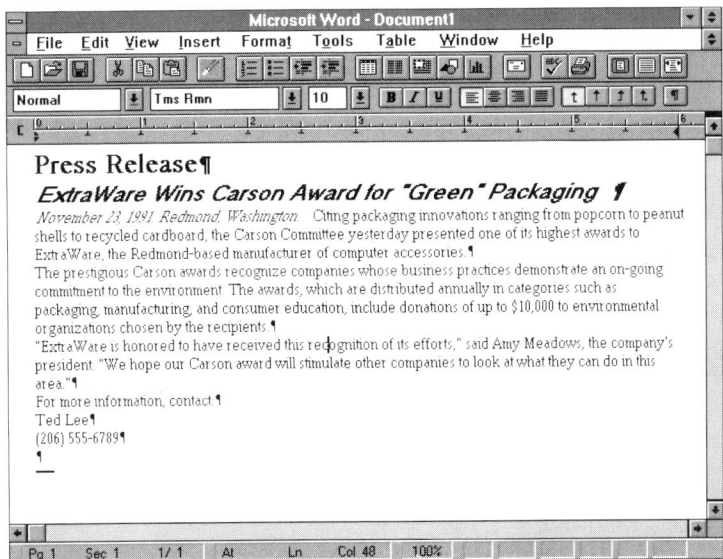

Try applying a couple of formats to the "contact" lines at the bottom of the press release:

1. Move the pointer into the selection bar adjacent to the line that begins *For more information*, and drag down to select the last three lines in the press release.
2. Click the Bold button to make all three lines bold.
3. Select *Ted Lee*, click the Size-box arrow, and select 12. The result is shown on the next page.

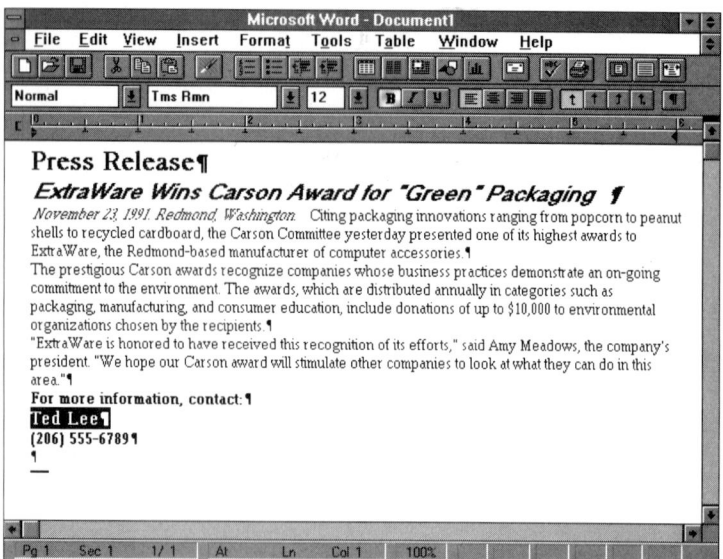

The Ribbon always reflects the formats of the selected text. If no text is selected, the Ribbon reflects the formats of the character to the left of the insertion point, except when the insertion point is at the beginning of a paragraph, in which case the Ribbon reflects the character to the right. Watch the Ribbon as you follow these steps:

1. Press Ctrl-Home to move the insertion point to the first character in the document. The Ribbon indicates that the formatting of the character to the right of the insertion point is 18-point Times Roman Bold.
2. Press the Down Arrow to move to the next line. The settings on the Ribbon change to 14-point Helvetica Bold Italic.
3. Continue pressing the Down Arrow key and observing the changes on the Ribbon, until you get to the phone number line.
4. Press End to move to the end of the last line. Then hold down Ctrl and Shift and press the Up Arrow key until the three paragraphs that tell who to contact for more information are selected. The Ribbon indicates that these paragraphs are formatted in Times Roman Bold but the Size setting is blank, as shown here:

Chapter 1 Word Basics: Writing a Press Release

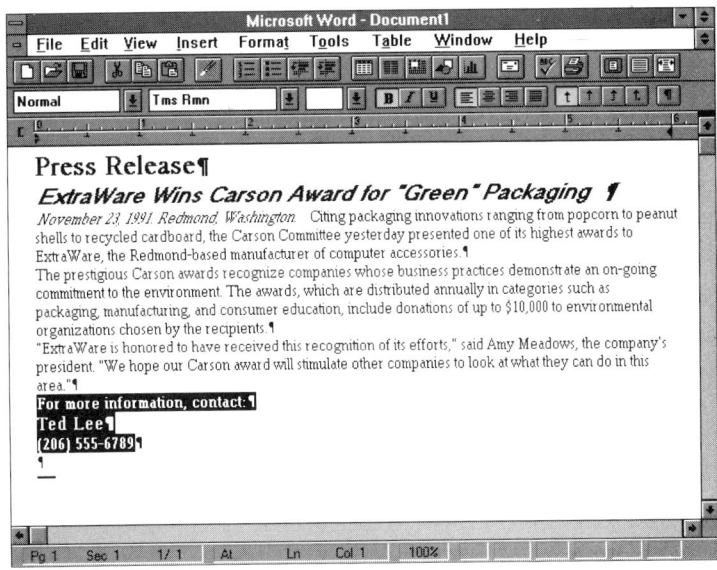

If you select a chunk of text that has more than one font or size, the corresponding Ribbon setting is blank. A selection with mixed character formatting causes some buttons on the Ribbon to appear "hollow."

We've changed the character formatting of parts of the press release. Now let's take a look at the effects produced by the alignment buttons:

1. With the last three paragraphs of the press release still selected, click the Right Align button to right-align all three lines at once.

2. Press Ctrl-Home to move the insertion point to the top of the press release. Then hold down Shift and press the Down Arrow key twice to select the two headings.

3. Click the Center button to center both headings.

4. Press the Right Arrow key to move to the start of the next line. Hold down Ctrl and Shift and press the Down Arrow key three times to highlight the main text of the press release. (Neither the headings nor the contact information should be highlighted.)

5. Click the Justify button to tell Word to spread out the text so that the lines fill the space between the left and right margins. Click anywhere in the text area to remove the highlighting so that you can see the results shown on the next page.

Right-aligning text

Centering text

Justifying text

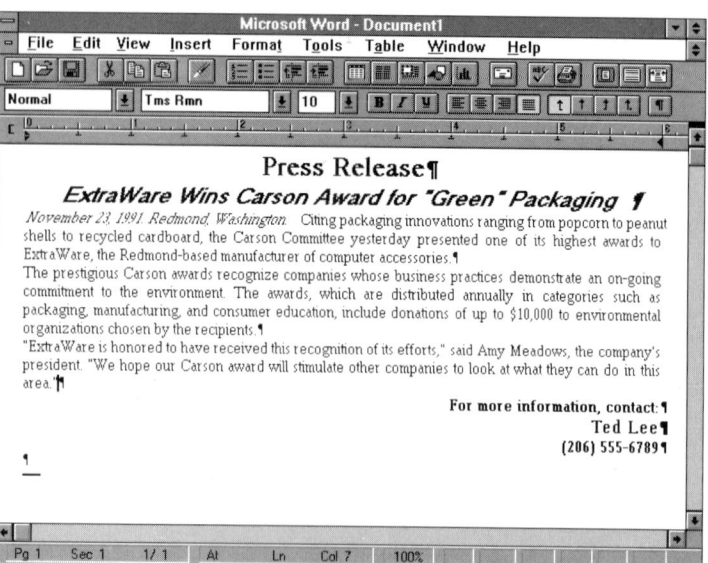

The Ruler You use the Ruler below the Ribbon to set indents, tabs, column widths, and margins. We explore these features in later chapters. At the left end of the Ruler is the ruler scale symbol, which you use to switch the ruler between three ruler scales: paragraph, table, and margin. The default is the paragraph scale. (We talk more about the table scale on page 92.)

Using the Menu Commands

When there is no button equivalent of a command on the Toolbar or Ribbon, or when you want to use a command with something other than the default settings, you can choose the command from the menus at the top of the window. Because this procedure is the same for all Windows applications, we assume that you are familiar with it and we provide only a quick review here. If you are a new Windows user, we suggest that you spend a little time becoming familiar with the mechanics of menus, commands, and dialog boxes before proceeding.

Choosing commands

To choose a command from a menu, you first click the name of the menu in the menu bar. When the menu drops down, you simply click the name of the command you want. From the keyboard, you can press Alt to activate the menu bar and then press the underlined letter on the name of the menu you want. To move from one open menu to another, use the Left and Right Arrow keys. When you have located the command you want, simply press its underlined letter, or press the Down Arrow key to highlight the desired command and then press Enter.

Some command names are displayed in gray letters, indicating that you can't choose the commands. For example, the Paste command on the Edit menu appears in gray until you use the Cut or Copy command, and the Cut and Copy commands appear in gray until you select some text.

Some command names are followed by an ellipsis (...), indicating that you must supply more information before Word can carry out the command. When you choose one of these commands, Word displays a dialog box. You can then give the necessary information by typing in a text box or by selecting options from list boxes, drop-down list boxes, or groups of check boxes and option buttons. Clicking one of the command buttons—usually OK—closes the dialog box and carries out the command according to your specifications. Clicking Cancel closes the dialog box and also cancels the command. Other command buttons might be available to refine the original command or to open other dialog boxes with more options.

Dialog boxes

Let's run through the steps for choosing a command and do some useful exploring at the same time.

1. Click View on the menu bar to display this menu, which provides commands for customizing the screen display. For example, the first three commands are mutually exclusive choices that determine how Word displays your documents. The Draft command toggles the first two views between a WYSIWYG (What You See Is What You Get) display and a draft display that shows no character formatting. Because we cover many of the features related to these commands elsewhere in the book, we won't discuss them here. For now, let's just play with the commands that affect screen layout.

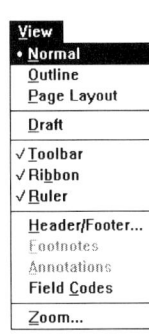

2. Choose the Toolbar command from the View menu. The Toolbar disappears.

Turning off the Toolbar and Ribbon

3. Next, choose the Ribbon command to turn off the Ribbon. Notice while the View menu is pulled down that Toolbar no longer has a check mark beside it, indicating that the Toolbar is turned off.

Turning off the Ruler

4. Choose the Ruler command from the View menu to turn off the Ruler. Your "naked" screen looks like this:

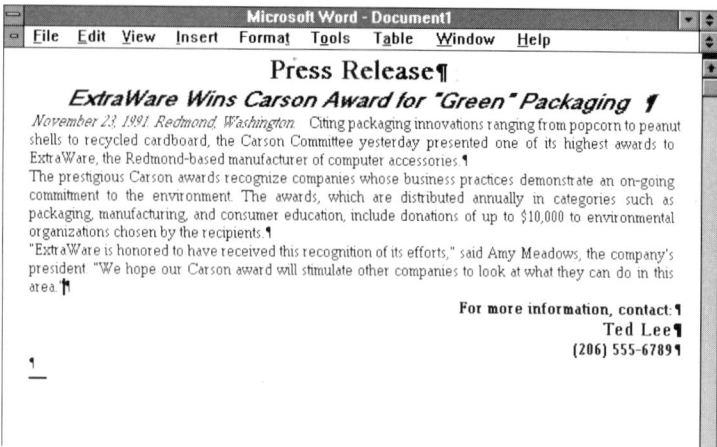

When you are working with a long document or have multiple documents displayed at one time, you might want to turn off these features so that you can see more of your text at one time. When you quit Word, many of the settings that control the appearance of the screen are stored in a file called WINWORD.INI in the directory containing Word. (This file is *not* WIN.INI, which is stored in the WINDOWS directory.) The next time you start Word, the stored settings are used, so the screen usually looks as it did when you left it.

5. Choose the Options command from the bottom of the Tools menu to display a dialog box something like this:

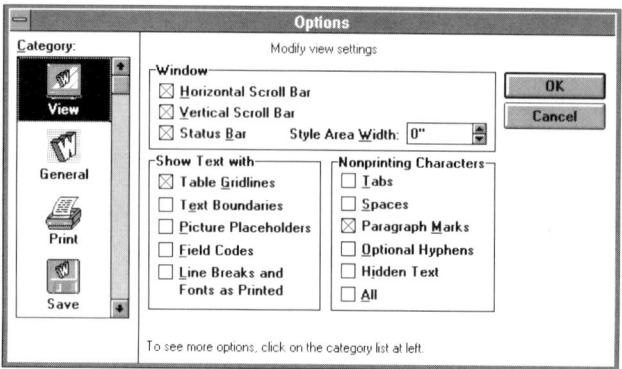

(If the View icon is not highlighted on the left side of this dialog box, click it to highlight it.) By selecting

Chapter 1 Word Basics: Writing a Press Release   15

various options in this dialog box, you can control the display of many different screen elements.

6. Turn off the Status Bar option in the Window section of the dialog box (there should be no X in its check box). Then turn off the All option in the Nonprinting Characters section, and click OK. (You can also turn the display of specific nonprinting symbols on and off from this dialog box.) As you can see here, Word turns off the status bar at the bottom of the screen, giving you a little more room for text, and also turns off the display of nonprinting symbols:

Turning off the status bar

Turning nonprinting symbols on and off

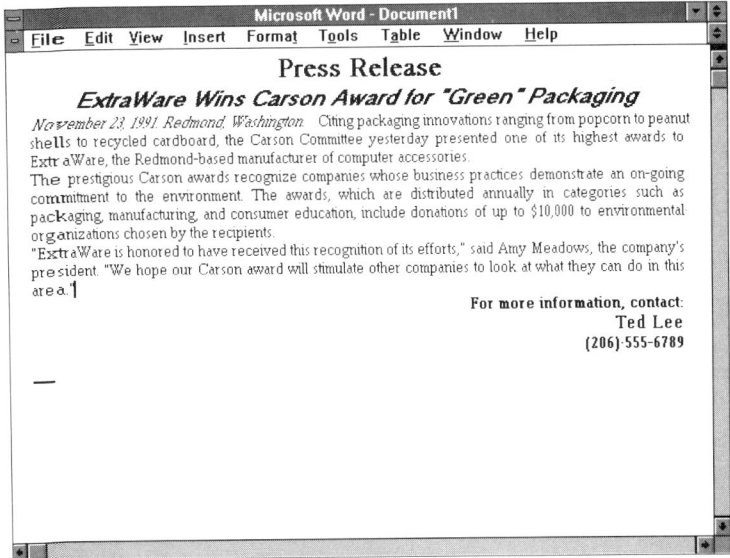

These symbols can sometimes be helpful when you are editing documents, because they show you where you have inserted characters such as spaces, tabs, and paragraph marks. (You insert a paragraph mark every time you hit the Enter key.)

7. Choose the Toolbar, Ribbon, and Ruler commands from the View menu. Then choose Options from the Tools menu, turn the status bar and nonprinting symbols back on, and click OK.

Turning on the Toolbar, Ribbon, and Ruler

If the nonprinting symbols annoy or confuse you, click the ¶ button at the right end of the Ribbon to turn them all off.

Using Keyboard Shortcuts

Although you can get by in Word using only the keyboard, frankly we don't know why you would want to. Using a mouse makes working with any Windows application much easier, and Word is no exception. However, if you prefer to use the keyboard, you can access many Word commands by using keyboard shortcuts. Here are a couple of useful ones:

1. Press Ctrl-5 (use the 5 key on the numeric keypad) to select the entire document.
2. Press Ctrl-O (the letter *O*) to put an extra line of space between all the paragraphs.
3. Press End to move to the end of the selection, press the Left Arrow key to move the insertion point to the line containing the phone number, and then press Ctrl-O (zero) to close up *Ted Lee* and the phone number.

Open spacing

Closed spacing

List of shortcuts

Word's list of shortcuts is extensive, and it would take a lot of space to reproduce it here. For more information about keyboard shortcuts, choose Help Keyboard from the Help menu, or choose Help Index and search on Shortcut.

Saving Documents

Now would be a good time to save the press release so that it is available for future use. To save a new document, you choose Save As from the File menu. Word displays a dialog box in which you specify the name of the document. Thereafter, clicking the Save button saves the document without displaying the dialog box, because the document already has a name. Let's save the document now on your screen:

Saving a new document

1. Choose Save As from the File menu. Word displays the Save As dialog box:

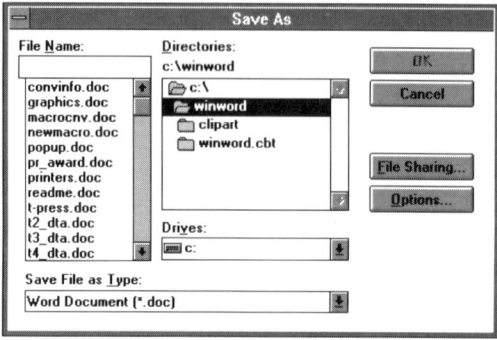

2. Type *pr_award* in the File Name text box. There's no need to supply an extension; Word automatically uses DOC if you don't specify something else.

Chapter 1   Word Basics: Writing a Press Release

3. Leave the other text boxes empty, and click OK. Word closes the Save As dialog box and displays a Summary Info dialog box like this one:

    ```
    ┌─────────────── Summary Info ───────────────┐
    │ File Name:  PR_AWARD.DOC          [  OK  ] │
    │ Directory:  C:\WINWORD            [Cancel] │
    │ Title:      [                  ]           │
    │ Subject:    [                  ] [Statistics...] │
    │ Author:     [Steve Lambert     ]           │
    │ Keywords:   [                  ]           │
    │ Comments:   [                  ]           │
    │             [                  ]           │
    └────────────────────────────────────────────┘
    ```

    By default, when you save a new document Word assumes you also want to store identifying information that will later help you find the file. Filling in summary information might seem time-consuming and irrelevant now, when you have only one file to deal with. However, after you have accumulated many files in several directories, you might well find yourself relying on this information to quickly locate the file you need. You'll want to get in the habit now of filling in the Summary Info dialog box, using as many of the text boxes as you can and being as precise as possible about the contents of this particular file.   ← *Summary information*

4. Word automatically fills in the name of the person who installed the program. Fill in the Title text box by typing *Carson Award Press Release*, and the Subject box by typing *Carson award*.

5. Click the Statistics button to display this dialog box: ← *Displaying document statistics*

    ```
    ┌─────────────── Document Statistics ───────────────┐
    │ File Name:         PR_AWARD.DOC           [  OK  ] │
    │ Directory:         C:\WINWORD                      │
    │ Template:          C:\WINWORD\NORMAL.DOT  [Update] │
    │ Title:             Carson Award Press Release      │
    │ Created:           11/30/91 12:37 AM               │
    │ Last saved:        11/30/91 12:37 AM               │
    │ Last saved by:     Steve Lambert                   │
    │ Revision number:   2                               │
    │ Total editing time: 37 Minutes                     │
    │ Last printed:                                      │
    │ As of last update:                                 │
    │   # of pages:      1                               │
    │   # of words:      200                             │
    │   # of characters: 945                             │
    └────────────────────────────────────────────────────┘
    ```

    As you can see, Word keeps track of when the document was created and revised; how long you have worked on this document; and the number of pages, words, and characters.

6. Click OK twice to close the dialog boxes and attach the summary information to the file.

When you return to the document window, notice that the name PR_AWARD.DOC has replaced Document1 in the document's title bar.

Saving existing documents

From now on, you can click the Save button any time you want to save changes to this document. Because Word knows the name of the document, it simply saves the document by overwriting the previous version with the new version.

Preserving the previous version

If you want to save the changes you have made to a document but preserve the previous version, you can assign the new version a different name by choosing the Save As command from the File menu, entering the new name in the File Name text box, and clicking OK. If you want to change the information stored with the file, simply choose Summary Info from the File menu to display the Summary Info dialog box, make your changes, and click OK.

Changing summary information

Retrieving Existing Documents

To give you an opportunity to practice moving around and selecting text in a longer document, let's open one of the documents that came with Word. The next few graphics are based on the file called README.DOC that was shipped with Word for Windows version 2.0. If you don't have this file, you can open any other DOC file that came with your Word disks and follow along.

To open the README.DOC file, follow these steps:

Opening a document

1. Click the Open button on the Toolbar. Word displays a dialog box something like this one:

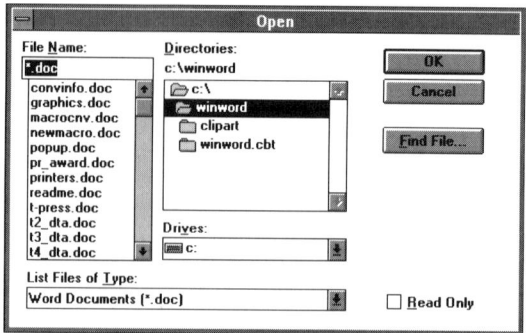

Chapter 1 Word Basics: Writing a Press Release

The filenames in the File Name list box are those with the DOC extension in the current directory, whose path is displayed below the word *Directories*.

2. If the file you want is not stored in the current directory, you need to switch to the correct directory before you can select the file. Double-click a directory to display that directory's DOC files in the File Name list box and its subdirectories in the Directories list box. Double-click a subdirectory to display its files and subdirectories, and so on.

3. When you have located the README.DOC file, open it by double-clicking its name. Word loads this file:

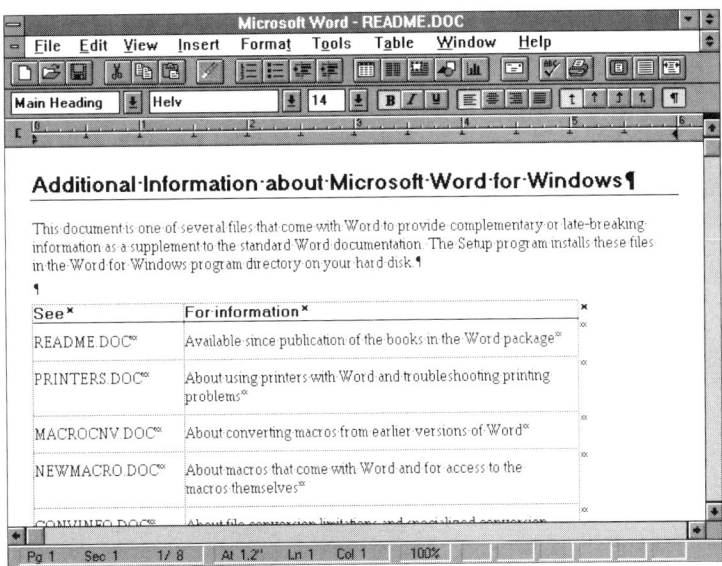

Creating New Documents

You now have two documents open on your screen, though PR_AWARD.DOC is totally obscured by README.DOC. For good measure, let's open a third document, this time a brand new one. Follow these steps:

1. Click New on the Toolbar or choose the New command from the Edit menu.

That's all there is to it. A new document called Document2 is displayed on your screen, on top of PR_AWARD.DOC and README.DOC.

Opening a new document

Manipulating Windows

Now that we have a few windows to play with, we'll pause here to review some window basics. Being able to work with more than one document open at a time is useful, especially if you need to use the same information in different documents. For example, you might use roughly the same text in a press release, in a memo to employees, and in a newsletter to clients. Follow these steps to see how easy it is to move from one document to another:

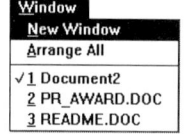

1. Open the Window menu to display its commands. As you can see, the three open documents are listed at the bottom of the menu, with a check mark beside Document2 to indicate that its window is active.
2. Choose PR_AWARD.DOC from the list of open documents. Word brings the press release to the top of the stack of windows.
3. Choose Arrange All from the Window menu. Word arranges the three open documents so that they each occupy about a third of the screen, like this:

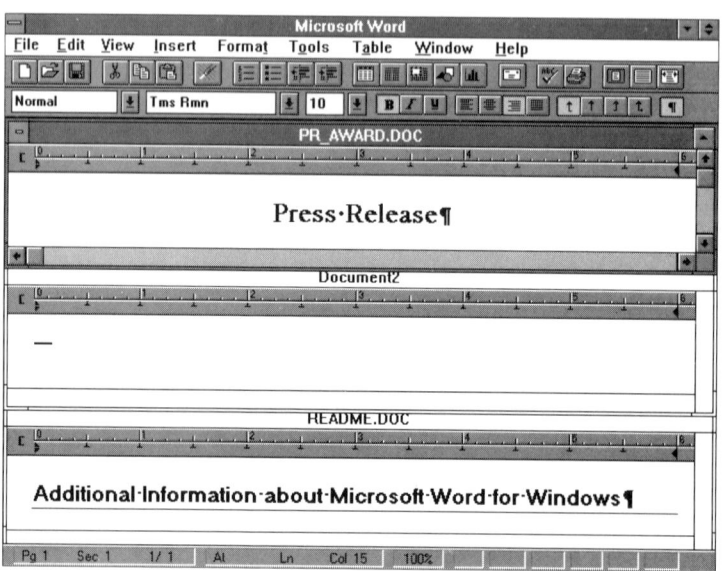

4. Click anywhere in README.DOC to activate it. Notice that the title bar of the active document is darker than the other two title bars and that scroll bars appear only in the active window. Any entries you make and most commands you choose will affect only the active document.

Chapter 1 Word Basics: Writing a Press Release

5. Click the README.DOC window's Maximize button. The window expands to fill the screen, completely obscuring the other two documents.
6. Choose the New Window command from the Window menu. Word opens a window that displays a second view of the active document, allowing you to see one part of the document while you edit another. The new window's title bar reads README.DOC:2.   *Opening a second view*
7. Click the Window menu. The original README.DOC file has become README.DOC:1 and is followed by README.DOC:2. Close the menu by clicking anywhere outside it.

Here's another way to see two parts of the same document at the same time:

1. Move the pointer to the thin black box, called the split box, just above the up scroll arrow in the vertical scroll bar. The pointer changes into a double horizontal bar with up and down arrows.   *Splitting a window*
2. Drag the split box downward to the position at which you want to split the README.DOC:2 window into panes. When you release the mouse button, your screen looks like this:

Notice that you now have two vertical scroll bars, one for each "pane."

Scrolling panes independently

3. In the bottom pane, click the vertical scroll bar below the scroll box. Notice that the text in the bottom pane scrolls, while the text in the top pane remains stationary.
4. To get rid of the pane, drag the split box back to the top of the screen or double-click the split box.

These simple techniques work equally well no matter how many documents you have open. (You can have nine files open at one time, but we've found that three is the practical limit if you want to be able to see them all at the same time and do useful work.)

Closing Documents

When you've finished working with a document, it's wise to close it to conserve your computer's memory for the work at hand. We'll use one way to close README.DOC:2 and another to close README.DOC:1.

1. With README.DOC:2 still active, choose Close from the Control menu at the left end of the menu bar (*not* the title bar). Word then closes the second view of the document. The title bar of README.DOC:1 reverts to plain old README.DOC to indicate that it is the only window displaying this document.
2. With README.DOC active, choose Close from the File menu. (If you have made inadvertent changes to the document, Word asks whether you want to save the document. Click No.)

Now only the press release and Document2 are still open on your screen.

Printing Documents

For all the talk in the popular press about a paperless office, the end product of a word-processing session is usually a printed document, whether you are writing a letter, a report, or a simple press release like the one we've developed in this chapter. Before you print from Word for the first time, you will need to check that your printer setup is correct. And before you print any document, you will want to check that all its elements are in place by using Word's Print Preview feature. Then printing is usually a simple matter of choosing the Print command from the File menu, setting a few options, and clicking OK. If you can print from any other Windows application, you should have no trouble printing from Word.

Setting Up for Printing

When you installed Windows, you indicated the printers you wanted to use. These printers are available from within Word, but you can use only one printer at a time. You select this printer as follows:

1. Choose Print Setup from the File menu. Word displays a dialog box like this one:

   ← Selecting a printer

   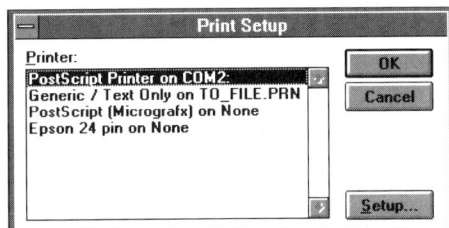

2. If more than one printer is listed in the Printer list box, select the one you want to use, and then click Setup to display this dialog box:

   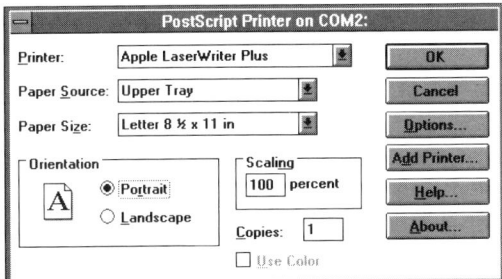

   You can use these settings to specify the paper source, paper size, and orientation you want to use as the defaults for all print operations. (You can override these defaults as well as select other options by choosing Page Setup from the Format menu for individual documents.)

3. Make any changes you need to make, click OK to return to the Print Setup dialog box, and then click OK again.

Previewing Documents

The press release you have created is only one page long and it has no headers or footers (see page 108 for information about headers and footers). However, it is worth checking even a document this small in Print Preview to get an idea of how it will look on the page when it is printed. Follow these steps to preview the press release:

Print Preview

1. Choose Print Preview from the File menu. Word displays the entire page, like this:

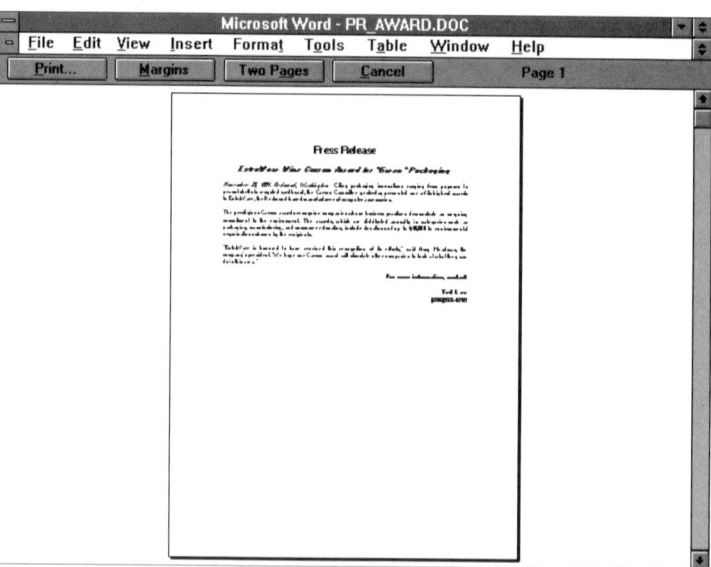

Switching views

2. Your display might show one or two pages. Switch views by clicking the One Page or Two Pages buttons.

Displaying margins

3. Click the Margins button to have Word indicate the document's margins with dotted lines. You can select these lines and move them to adjust the margins.
4. Click the Close button (which is called Cancel until you change something) to return to Normal view.

Straightforward Printing

You can print directly from Print Preview by clicking the Print button. When you are not in Print Preview, here's how you print your document:

Quick printing

1. Click the Print button on the Toolbar. Word prints the active document with the settings currently specified in the Print dialog box.

Chapter 1 Word Basics: Writing a Press Release

2. When printing is complete, choose Print from the File menu. Word displays a dialog box like this one:

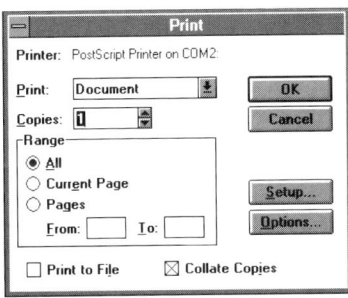

The settings in this dialog box control print operations you initiate by clicking the Print button. If you want to change the number of copies or the range of pages that will be printed, you must do it here. For example, if you change the number of copies to 2 and then click OK, Word prints two copies of the press release. If you then click the Print button, Word uses the settings in the Print dialog box and prints two more copies of the press release.

Changing the number of copies

3. Click Cancel to close the dialog box with the number of copies still set to 1.

Next, rather than explain the other printing options in detail here, we'll show you how to find out about them.

Getting Help

This has been a whistle-stop tour of Word, and you might not remember everything we've covered. If you forget how to carry out a particular task, help is never far away.

Looking at the Status Bar

One often-overlooked source of help is the status bar. While you work on your document, the status bar displays such information as (from left to right) the page number and section number, how far you are from the beginning of the document (as a percentage), how far you are from the top of the page, the line and column number, and the zoom percentage. (All these items of information, except zoom, are based on the position of the insertion point.) When you highlight a command on a menu, the status bar displays a description of the command. You can search through the menus, highlighting the commands and checking their descriptions in the status bar.

Using the Help Program

You can access Word's Help program in two ways: By choosing commands from the Help menu and by using a keyboard shortcut to access information about a highlighted command. Let's look at both methods:

1. Choose Help Index from the Help menu to display a list of topics concerning almost every aspect of Word.
2. Scroll through the index, and select Menu Commands.

Help with printing

3. From the list of commands, select Print. Word displays this Help screen:

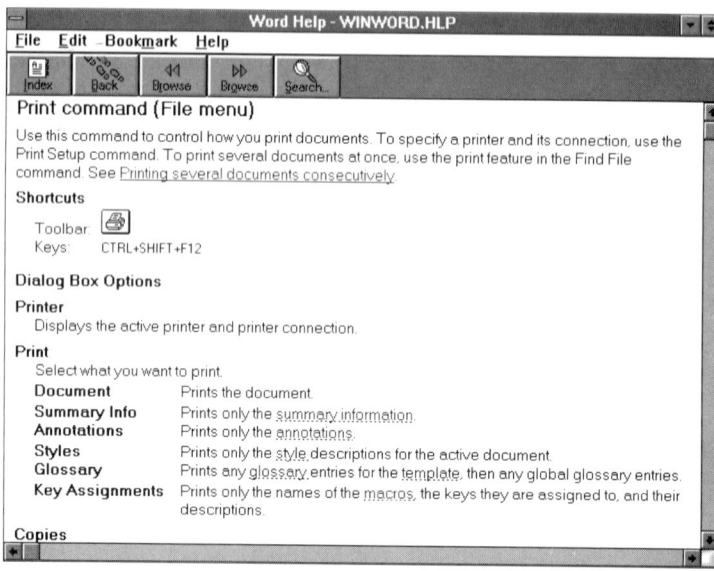

4. Scroll through the information about the Print command, and then experiment with the Browse Backward and Browse Forward buttons. When you're finished, click Back until you return all the way to the index.

Searching

5. Click the Search button. Word displays this dialog box:

Chapter 1 Word Basics: Writing a Press Release

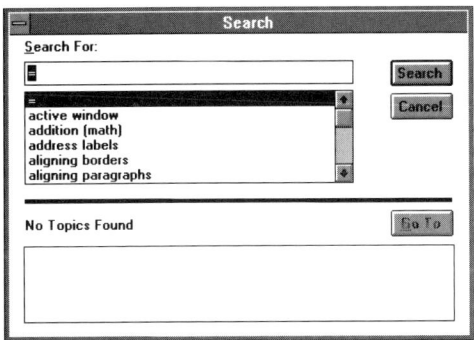

6. In turn, press the P, R, and I keys. Word scrolls the Search For list to display topics beginning with *pri*.
7. Scroll the list box so that you can select *printing: paper settings*. If you now click the Search button, Word displays a list of all the topics related to this subject. You can select one of the topics and then click the Go To button to jump directly to that Help screen.
8. Choose Exit from the screen's File menu to leave Help.

You can also jump immediately to the appropriate Help screen to get information about the task at hand. For example, let's see how you would remind yourself of how to use the Print command on the File menu:

1. Highlight the Print command on the File menu, and without releasing the mouse button, press F1. Word displays the same Help screen you saw earlier.
2. Double-click the Control-menu icon in the top-left corner of the Help screen to close the screen.

Quitting Word

Well, that's it for the basic tour. We'll finish up by showing you how to end a Word session.

1. Choose Exit from the File menu.
2. If Word asks whether you want to save the changes you have made to the press release, click Yes.

We'll work with the press-release document again in Chapter 3. In Chapter 2, we cover ways of organizing and editing your documents.

2

Letter-Perfect Documents: Producing a Company Backgrounder

Creating Longer Documents   30
   Developing an Outline   30
      Adjusting Headings   32
      Adding Text   33
   Viewing Parts of the Document   34
   Organizing the Document   36
Using the Glossary   37
   Creating Glossary Entries   37
   Inserting Glossary Entries   38
   Modifying Glossary Entries   40
   Deleting Glossary Entries   40
   Saving the Glossary   41
Editing Basics   41
   Overtyping Text   41
   Copying and Moving Text   42
   Deleting Text   43
   Undoing Commands   44
Finding and Replacing   44
   Finding Text   44
   Replacing Text   47
Checking Spelling   49
   Spell-Checking an Entire Document   49
   Spell-Checking a Selection   51
   Creating and Using Custom Dictionaries   51
Checking Grammar   52

Heading styles
Page 31

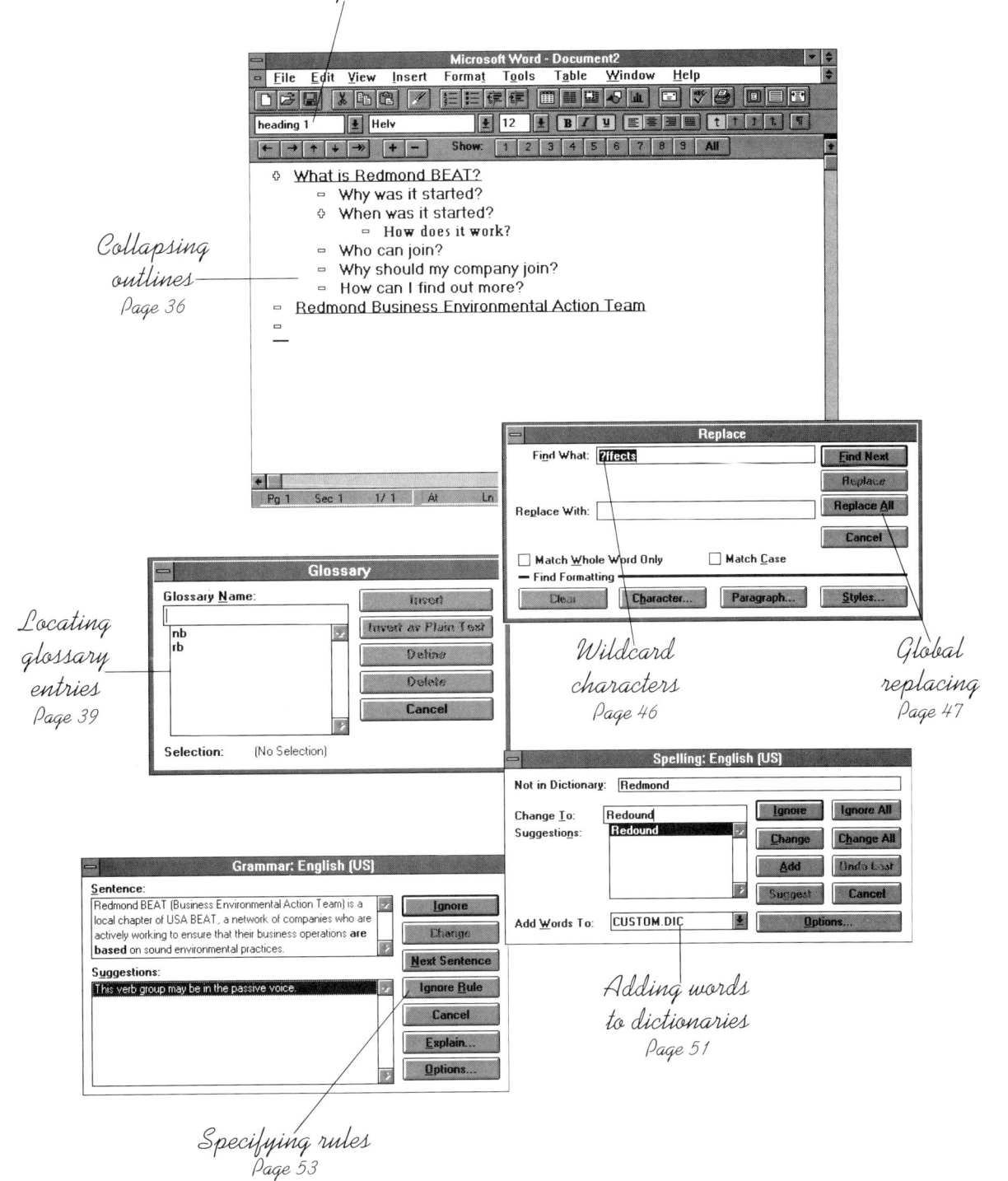

Collapsing outlines
Page 36

Locating glossary entries
Page 39

Wildcard characters
Page 46

Global replacing
Page 47

Adding words to dictionaries
Page 51

Specifying rules
Page 53

With Word for Windows, you can apply fancy formats and add graphics and special effects to increase the impact of a document. But all the frills in the world won't compensate for poor organization and spelling or grammatical errors. That's why this chapter focuses on the Word tools that help you develop and refine the content of your documents. First we look at Word's outlining and glossary features, and then we cover basic editing skills, as well as searching and replacing. Finally, we discuss spell-checking and grammar-checking. By the end of this chapter, you'll know how to ensure that your organization is solid and your writing is correct, and you'll be ready to learn how to make your documents look good.

Creating Longer Documents

When a document has headings as well as ordinary text, using Word's outlining feature is not only the simplest way to get started but it can also speed up the process of formatting the document after you've written it. We realize that we will never convince some of you that it is worth taking the time to outline a document, but others of you might decide that outlining is just the tool for creating certain kinds of documents.

Follow along as we use Word's outlining feature to create a "backgrounder" for an association called Redmond Business Environmental Action Team (BEAT). Backgrounders provide basic information about a company or organization, and they are often mailed out with press releases and other promotional materials. You can follow our instructions to create our example backgrounder or you can create one for your own company.

Developing an Outline

Most people are accustomed to thinking of outlining as the process that precedes the writing of lengthy documents. With Word, however, outlining is not a separate process, but simply another way of looking at your document. If you use Word's outlining feature to create a traditional outline, you can later switch to Outline view at any time to get an overview of your document.

Chapter 2 Letter-Perfect Documents: Producing a Company Backgrounder 31

In this section, we'll create the outline for a new document, and then we'll gradually expand the outline. Let's get started:

1. Click the New button to open a new blank document, and choose Outline from the View menu to display the outline screen. In place of the Ruler, you now see a row of buttons that allow you to organize your document and assign levels to the information you enter.

Creating an outline

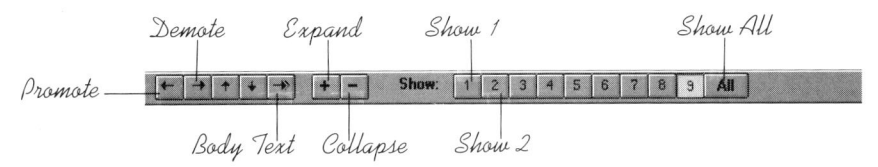

Promote *Demote* *Expand* *Show 1* *Show All*
Body Text *Collapse* *Show 2*

2. Type *What is Redmond BEAT?*, and press Enter. Word assumes that the first paragraph of the new document is a first-level heading and that the next paragraph will be a first-level heading as well. This information is stored with the paragraph symbol Word inserts when you press Enter.

3. Type *Why was it started?*, and press Enter. Your outline now looks like this:

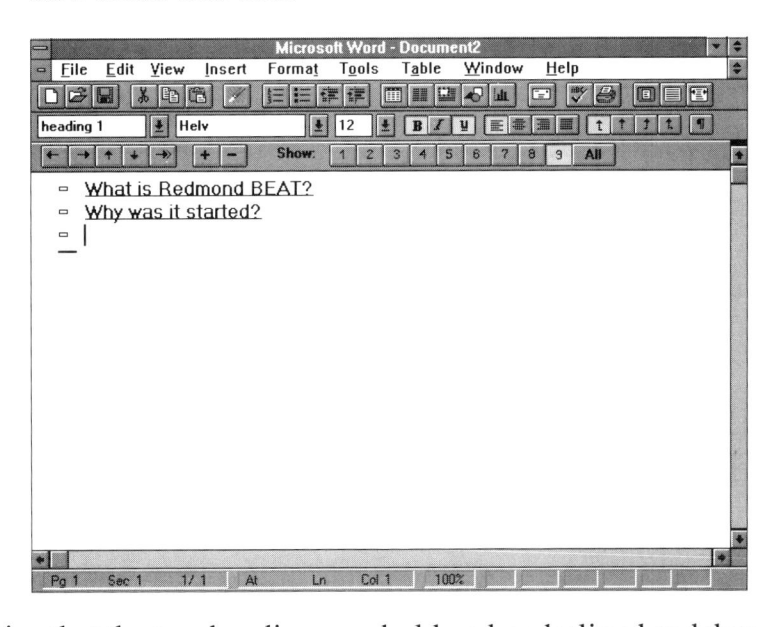

- What is Redmond BEAT?
- Why was it started?

Notice that the two headings are bold and underlined and that *heading 1* appears in the style box. With Word, you can create up to nine heading levels, called *heading 1* through *heading 9*. Also notice the minus icons next to the headings you've just typed; they indicate that the headings have no sub-headings or text.

Heading styles

Minus icons

Demoting headings

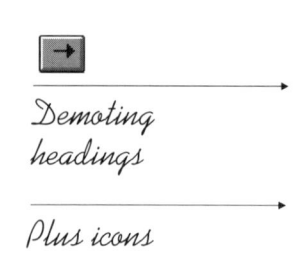

Plus icons

Promoting headings

Adjusting Headings You adjust the level of a heading by using the Demote and Promote buttons, like this:

1. Move the insertion point into the second heading, and click the Demote button. Word changes the appearance of the heading, indents it, and displays *heading 2* in the style box. The minus icon next to *What is Redmond BEAT?* changes to a plus icon to indicate that it now has a subordinate heading.
2. Press the End key to move to the end of the heading, and press Enter.
3. Type *When was it started?*, and press Enter. The new heading looks the same and is indented to the same level as the preceding heading.
4. Click the Demote button again, type *How does it work?*, and then press Enter. Word indents this third-level heading another half inch to indicate that it is subordinate to the preceding second-level heading.
5. Type *Who can join?*, and then click the Promote button to change the heading from a *heading 3* to a *heading 2*. As demonstrated, you can type a heading and then adjust its level, or you can specify the level and subsequently enter the heading.
6. Add two more second-level headings: *Why should my company join?* and *How can I find out more?*. Be sure to press Enter after the second one.
7. Click the Promote button, and add a first-level heading: *Redmond Business Environmental Action Team*.

Demoting/promoting text	Draft view	Speedy navigation
If you select a text paragraph in Outline view and then click the Promote or Demote button, Word converts the selected text to the same level as the immediately superior or inferior heading. ♦	If you think it would be easier to work with the outline without all its formatting, you can switch to Draft view by choosing the Draft command from the View menu. To redisplay the outline's formatting, choose the command again. ♦	To move quickly and easily around an outlined document: **1.** Choose Outline to display the document in Outline view. **2.** Collapse the outline by clicking one of the Show buttons. **3.** Highlight the heading or text paragraph you want to move to. **4.** Scroll the highlighted text to the top of your screen. **5.** Display the text in Normal view. ♦

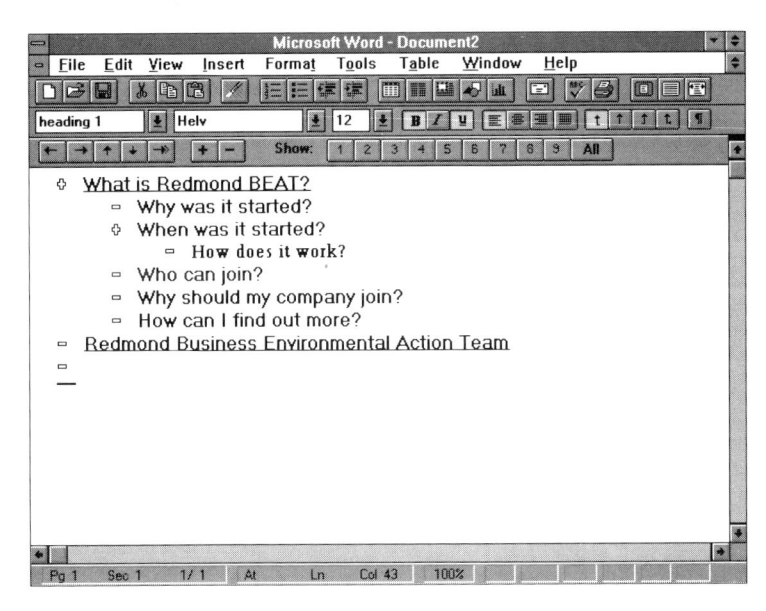

Chapter 2 Letter-Perfect Documents: Producing a Company Backgrounder

8. Now save the document by clicking the Save button, specifying *bkground.doc* as the name of the file, and then specifying Redmond BEAT in the Title box of the Summary Info dialog box.

Saving the outline

In Chapter 3, we'll use the entries in the Summary Info dialog box to help us find this file.

Adding Text As you can see, using Outline view helps you see the relationships between topics. Now let's add some text to a few of these headings. You can add text in Outline view, or you can switch back to Normal view to add text.

Normal view

1. Click the Normal View button, click an insertion point after the question mark at the end of the *What is Redmond BEAT?* heading, press Enter, and type the following:

   Redmond BEAT (Business Environmental Action Team) is a local chapter of National BEAT, a network of companies who are actively working to ensure that their business operations are based on sound environmental practices.

   Notice that the paragraph you just typed is not formatted as a *heading 1* entry, even though the insertion point was at the end of a *heading 1* entry when you pressed Enter.

2. Now choose Outline from the View menu, click an insertion point at the end of the third-level *How does*

it work? heading, press Enter, and type the following paragraph (including the errors marked in bold, so you will have some mistakes to correct later in the chapter):

Member companies agree to participate in two ongoing efforts: 1. They pledge to scrutinize **there** operations and, wherever possible, implement procedures that will minimize any adverse **affects** on the environment. 2. They agree to field-test new "**environmentlly** kind" products and services to evaluate their potential impact on both company costs and the environment.

Changing headings to body text

3. Because you are working in Outline view, Word assumes that the paragraph is a third-level heading. To demote the heading to body text, click the Body Text button.
4. Looking through the outline, you realize that the third-level *How does it work?* heading should really be a second-level heading. Select it, and click the Promote button. Word moves the heading to the left and reformats it to reflect its new status. It also moves the subordinate body text to the left so that the relationship between the heading and the text is maintained.
5. Now add another body-text paragraph. Click an insertion point at the end of the second-level *Why should my company join?* heading, press Enter, and type the following (again, include the error marked in bold):

Current members cite two main reasons for joining. Many companies are managed by people who were attracted to this area by **it's** natural beauty and who want to be part of the effort to preserve it. Other companies stress the potential advantages in today's competitive markets of being perceived as a "green" company by consumers who are increasingly environmentally aware.

6. Change this paragraph to body text by clicking the Body Text button.
7. Before going any further, save the document again.

Viewing Parts of the Document

Having created an outline, you can view your document at various levels by clicking the Show buttons. The Redmond BEAT backgrounder is fairly short and has only two heading levels, but experimenting with this document will give you an idea of how you might use these buttons to manage much longer documents.

1. Click the Show All button to display the entire document in Outline view.

   Entire outline

2. Now collapse the outline so that only the *heading 1* entries are visible by clicking the Show 1 button. Here's the result:

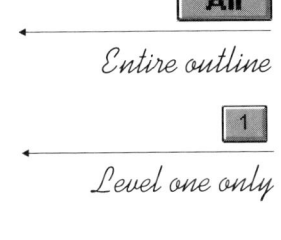

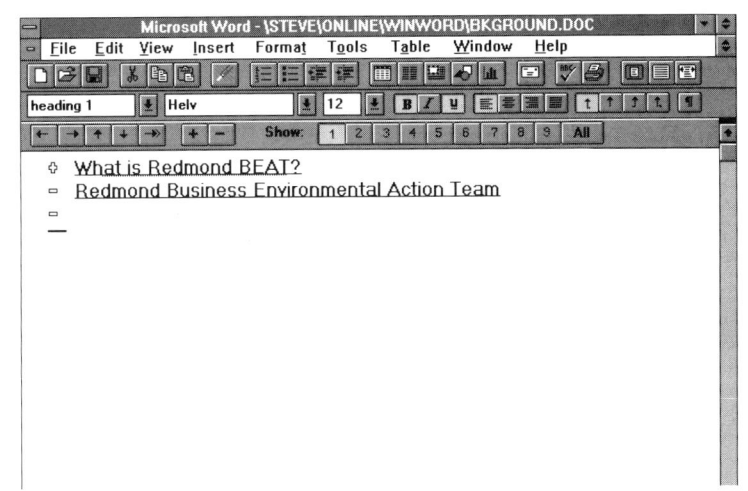

   Level one only

3. To expand the outline by one level, click the Show 2 button to display *heading 1* and *heading 2* entries. Now only the body text is hidden.

   Level one and two

Numbering topics

To number the headings in an outline: **1.** Select the headings you want to number. (Collapse the outline before you number it to number only the visible headings.) **2.** Choose the Bullets And Numbering command from the Tools menu. **3.** Click the Outline option, specify the numbering scheme you want to use (for example, Legal), and click OK. Word numbers each heading according to its level, but does not number body-text paragraphs. If you want to number text paragraphs, choose the Bullets And Numbering command in Normal view rather than Outline view. ♦

Deleting headings

To delete a heading from an outline, select the heading, and press Del. If you want to also delete the heading's subordinate headings and text, collapse the outline before you make your selection. Otherwise, expand the outline before you select the heading so that you can see exactly which paragraphs will be affected when you press Del. ♦

The Show buttons affect your entire outline. When working on a long document, you might want to use the Expand and Collapse buttons to expand only the part that you are working on. Here's how these buttons work:

Expanding outlines

Collapsing outlines

1. Click an insertion point in the *Why should my company join?* heading, and then click the Expand button. Word displays the body text you typed earlier.
2. Collapse the body text back under its heading by clicking the Collapse button.

You can also double-click the plus icon next to a heading to expand or collapse its subordinate headings or text.

Organizing the Document

Organizing a document is often a trial-and-error process. You list the major topics, add a few subtopics and some body text, and then start tinkering with the organization, moving some headings and changing the level of others until you are satisfied with the outline. We've already seen how to change heading levels. Rearranging headings is equally easy:

1. Click the plus icon next to the *How does it work?* heading to select the heading and its body text.
2. Drag the pointer (a four-way arrow) upward in the outline until the bar representing the heading is under *What is Redmond BEAT?*. When you release the mouse button, *How does it work?* moves to become the first second-level heading in the outline.
3. With the *How does it work?* heading still selected, click the Expand button to display the subordinate text, which has moved with the heading to its new location.
4. Select the minus icon next to the *Redmond Business Environmental Action Team* heading, and drag it to the very top of the document.
5. To make *What is Redmond BEAT?* a second-level heading, click an insertion point in it, and click the Demote button.
6. Next, click the Normal View button.
7. We'll continue to work with this document for the rest of this chapter, so save it now.

Next, we'll move on to discuss a Word feature that was designed with writing efficiency and consistency in mind.

Using the Glossary

Word's glossary is a storage place for text and graphics. Unlike the Clipboard, the glossary is saved from one Word session to the next, so you can store an entry in the glossary under a name and then insert it in any document at any time simply by using the name. A glossary entry can be as short as a single text character or as long as several pages of text or graphics, and it can include formatting. Once you get in the habit of using the glossary, you'll find it helpful not only as a time-saving device—you can reuse text and graphics instead of having to type and format them each time—but also as a way of ensuring accuracy and consistency.

Every industry has its jargon—some more complex than others. Any term that is long or difficult to type is a candidate for a glossary entry. For example, suppose you own a landscaping business. Just imagine how much time and effort you would save if you were able to insert a glossary entry with the name *pt*, instead of having to type and format *Populus tremuloides* (the botanical name for the aspen tree).

Creating Glossary Entries

For this example, we'll turn a couple of phrases we have already typed into glossary entries. Follow along as we add *Redmond BEAT* and *National BEAT* to Word's glossary.

1. At the start of the first text paragraph, select *Redmond BEAT*, and choose Glossary from the Edit menu to display this dialog box:

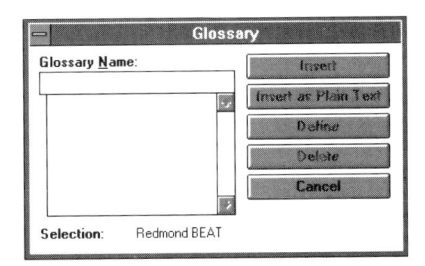

    Word displays the selected text at the bottom of the dialog box. If the selection is a graphic, Word displays a small box.

2. Type *rb* in the Glossary Name text box, and click the Define button. Word closes the dialog box.

3. Repeat steps 1 and 2 to store *National BEAT* in the glossary with the code *nb*.

Inserting Glossary Entries

Now let's use the entries we've just created as we write a few more paragraphs for the backgrounder.

1. Click an insertion point at the end of the *Why was it started?* heading, press Enter, and type the following (don't press the Spacebar after *rb*):

   The chartering of rb

Using the keyboard

2. Press F3. Word replaces *rb* with the *Redmond BEAT* glossary entry.

3. Continue typing the following paragraph, using the *rb*-F3 and *nb*-F3 sequences to insert *Redmond BEAT* and *National BEAT* where indicated. Be sure to type the error marked in bold exactly as you see it, and to include the **** characters, which are placeholders for information we'll add later.

   was spearheaded by William Henry, President of Creative GlassWorks. Struck by the incongruity between his family's efforts to recycle household waste and the fact that his company was sending several dumpsters of garbage to the landfill every month, Henry began looking for other ways to dispose of the packaging in which his company received raw materials. His questions caused one of his suppliers, ****, to explore alternative packaging methods. The result was less garbage in the Creative GlassWorks dumpsters at no additional cost and negligible other effects for either company. In the meantime, Henry learned about *nb*-F3, and a few months of persuasive **campaining** later, *rb*-F3 became the newest chapter of a rapidly growing national association.

4. Let's use the entries a few more times, so you can get a feel for what a time-saver the glossary can be. Click an insertion point at the end of the *When was it started?* heading, press Enter, and type

   nb-F3, which currently has 210 local chapters, was founded in 1987. *rb*-F3 was founded in 1990.

   Next, click an insertion point at the end of the *Who can join?* heading, press Enter, and type the following:

Membership in *rb-F3* is open to all companies licensed to do business in the city of Redmond. For more information, contact Ted Lee at ****.

Suppose you forget the code for a glossary entry. Does that mean you can't use the entry anymore? Not at all. Try this:

1. Click an insertion point at the end of the *How can I find out more?* heading, press Enter, and type *Come to a meeting* followed by a period and a space.
2. Choose Glossary from the Edit menu to display this Glossary dialog box:

Locating glossary entries

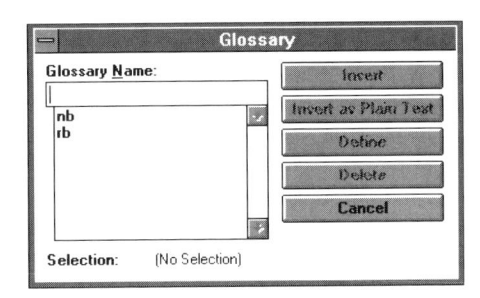

The codes in the list box serve as reminders of the entries you have created. You can select them in turn and check the bottom of the dialog box to see what each one represents.

3. Select *rb* from the list box, and click the Insert button. Word closes the dialog box and inserts the entry at the insertion point.

Glossary code rules

A glossary-entry code can be several words, but it cannot be more than 31 characters. You can use punctuation marks and special characters. Codes that begin with special characters appear at the end of the list in the Glossary dialog box. ♦

No duplicate codes

If you type a code that you have already used and then click the Define button, Word tells you that the code is assigned to another entry. Word considers uppercase to be the same as lowercase, so you cannot use *us* and *US* for two different entries. ♦

Entry formatting

Because Word stores a paragraph's formatting with the paragraph symbol, if you include a paragraph mark in a glossary entry, the entry retains its paragraph formatting when you insert it in a document. If the glossary entry doesn't include a paragraph symbol, the entry assumes the formatting of the paragraph in which you insert it. ♦

4. Finish typing the paragraph as follows:

   meets at 8:00 AM on the last Tuesday of every month in the Community Center.

Modifying Glossary Entries

Modifying a glossary entry is as easy as creating one from scratch. Suppose you want to change the *National BEAT* glossary entry to *USA BEAT*, but because you are in the habit of using the code *nb* to refer to the national association, you don't want to change the code. Follow these steps:

1. First click an insertion point after the *l* of *National* in the paragraph under the *When was it started?* heading, and press the Backspace key until the word *National* is deleted. Then type *USA* in its place.
2. Next, select *USA BEAT*, and choose Glossary from the Edit menu.
3. In the Glossary dialog box, click *nb*, the code for the glossary entry you want to replace. Word then displays the code in the Glossary Name text box and the entry itself at the bottom of the dialog box.
4. Click the Define button. After prompting for approval, Word replaces the old glossary entry with the new selection and closes the dialog box. From now on, typing *nb* and pressing F3 will insert *USA BEAT* instead of *National BEAT*.
5. Record your changes by saving the document.

The backgrounder contains two other references to National BEAT that also need updating. We'll leave these for now so that we can use them later as examples of how you can quickly substitute one text string for another.

Deleting Glossary Entries

Deleting a glossary entry is a simple matter of choosing the Glossary command to display the Glossary dialog box, selecting the code for the entry you want to delete, and clicking the Delete button. Word displays an alert box asking you to confirm the deletion. Click the Yes button to remove the specified entry.

Saving the Glossary

All the changes you make to the glossary during a Word session are stored in your computer's memory until you quit Word. When you choose Exit to leave the program, Word asks whether you want to save your changes. Let's run through this process now:

1. Choose Exit from the File menu. Word displays this dialog box:

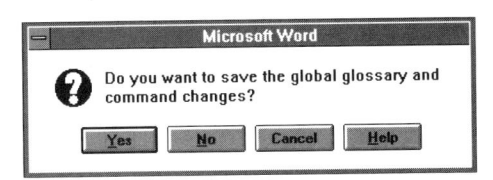

2. Click the Yes button. Word closes the dialog box, saves the glossary, and quits. If you click No, your changes to the glossary are lost, and if you click Cancel, Word stops the exit procedure.

Your glossary entries are stored as part of the specifications for the Normal template in a file called NORMAL.DOT. (For more information about templates, see page 105.) Word calls this glossary the global glossary because it is available for use with all documents.

Word's global glossary

Editing Basics

Most word-processing efforts, whether a note to yourself or an annual report, are created through an iterative process of typing and editing. In this section, we briefly cover some simple ways of revising documents. We'll make a few changes to the backgrounder to get a feel for what's involved.

Overtyping Text

By default, Word is in Insert mode, meaning that when you click an insertion point and begin typing, the characters you enter are inserted to the left of the insertion point, pushing any existing text to the right. Word can also operate in Overtype mode, meaning that when you click an insertion point and begin typing, each character you enter replaces an existing character.

Insert mode

Overtype mode

Let's experiment a bit with overtyping. Suppose Redmond BEAT was actually founded in 1989, not 1990. Here's how to make this simple correction:

1. If you are continuing from the previous section, start Word again, and open BKGROUND.DOC by choosing it from the bottom of the File menu, where Word lists the four most recently opened files.
2. Click an insertion point between the first and second 9s of 1990 under the *When was it started?* heading.
3. Press the Ins key. The letters *OVR* appear in the status bar to indicate that you are now in Overtype mode.
4. Type *8*, which overtypes the second 9, and then type *9*, which overtypes the 0, so that the entry now correctly reads *1989*.
5. Press the Ins key to turn off Overtype mode. This step is important; you might overtype valuable information if you forget it.

Turning on Overtype mode

Turning off Overtype mode

Copying and Moving Text

You can copy any amount of text within the same document or to a different document. Copy operations involve the use of two commands: Copy and Paste. Follow these steps:

1. Click an insertion point anywhere in the sentence that begins *For more information* under the *Who can join?* heading.
2. Press F8 three times—first to turn on Extend-Selection mode, second to highlight the word containing the insertion point, and third to highlight the sentence containing the selected word.
3. Click the Copy button on the Toolbar, or choose Copy from the Edit menu. Word stores a copy of the selected text in a temporary storage place in memory called the Clipboard.
4. Press Ctrl-End to move to the end of the document, and then move the insertion point to just after the last period in the preceding paragraph.
5. Press the Spacebar, and then click the Paste button or choose Paste from the Edit menu. Word inserts the copied sentence in the designated location, and your document now looks like this:

Copying text

Pasting text

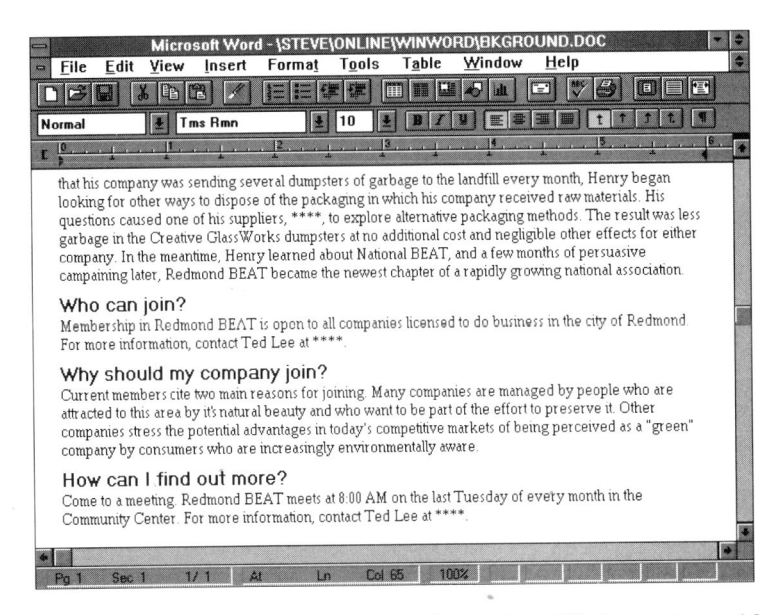

The original selection is still stored on the Clipboard, so if you needed to, you could paste another copy of the text without having to copy it again.

The procedure for moving text is almost identical to that for copying text, except that you use the Cut and Paste buttons. But there's another way to copy and move text. Try this technique, which is called drag-and-drop editing:

Drag-and-drop editing

1. Select the *When was it started?* heading and the following paragraph.
2. Point to the highlighted text, hold down the mouse button and when the mouse pointer changes to an arrow with a gray box below it, drag the pointer up to the beginning of the *Why was it started?* heading. When you release the mouse button, the selected text moves to the specified location. You have, in effect, transposed the *When was it started?* and *Why was it started?* sections.

If you hold down the Ctrl key while you drag the pointer, you copy the selected text instead of moving it.

Deleting Text

The Clipboard can hold only one selection at a time, and clicking either Copy or Cut replaces the Clipboard's contents with the new selection. Suppose that in the middle of the previous move operation, you realize that the sentence that begins *For more information* is now repeated in two sections of the backgrounder. You want to delete the occurrence after the *Who can join?* heading without disturbing the contents of the Clipboard. You could position the insertion point after the period and press Backspace; but here's an easier way:

1. With the insertion point in the first *For more information* sentence, press F8 three times to select the sentence.
2. Press the Del key. Word removes the sentence without storing it on the Clipboard.

Undoing Commands

For those occasions when you make an editing mistake, Word provides a safety net: the Undo command. As long as you click the Undo button or choose Undo before you carry out another editing task, including typing new characters, Word can undo your last editing action. Try this:

1. Press F8 four times to select the paragraph under the *Who can join?* heading, and then press Del. The paragraph is gone. Do you need to panic? No.
2. Click the Undo button, or choose Undo from the Edit menu. Word restores the paragraph as if nothing had happened.

Undoing a deletion

That quick tour of basic Word editing techniques should allow you to correct most mistakes, but before we leave the topic of editing, we need to cover two related features that allow you to make broad-based changes efficiently.

Finding and Replacing

With Word, you can search a document for specific characters, formats, or styles. You can also specify replacement characters, formats, or styles. Because we don't cover formats and styles until the next chapter, we focus here on finding and replacing text. For tips about finding and replacing styles, see page 75.

Finding Text

Finding a series of characters is easy. Being able to refine the search so that you locate precisely the characters you want

Chapter 2 Letter-Perfect Documents: Producing a Company Backgrounder

takes a little practice. But once you know how to use the options Word provides, you will have no trouble zeroing in on any series of characters.

Recall that while typing the Redmond BEAT backgrounder, you left the characters **** as placeholders for information that needed to be added later. Suppose you now need to locate the placeholders so that you can substitute the correct information. In a document as short as the backgrounder, you would have no difficulty locating ****. But if the current document were several pages long and several placeholders were involved, you would probably want to use the Find command to locate them. Here's how:

1. Press Ctrl-Home to move the insertion point to the top of the document.
2. Choose Find from the Edit menu. Word displays this dialog box:

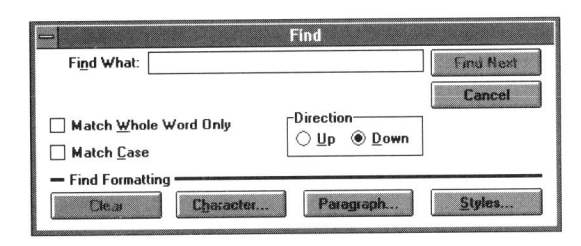

3. Enter **** in the Find What text box.
4. Leave the other options as they are, and click Find Next. Word searches the document, stopping when it locates the first occurrence of ****.
5. Click Cancel to close the dialog box, press Del to delete the placeholder, and then type *Jordon Manufacturing*.
6. Press Shift-F4 to repeat the Find command with the same Find What text and options as the previous search. Word locates the second ****.
7. Press Del, and type *555-6789*.

If you are searching a large document and you want to be sure that you have substituted the correct information for all the placeholders, you can press Shift-F4 to search again. Word searches to the end of the document and then asks whether to continue from the beginning of the document. Click Yes to have Word search from the beginning of the

Repeating a search

document. If Word does not find any occurrences of the Find What text, it displays another dialog box. Click OK to end the search.

Most of your searches will be as simple as this one was, but you can also refine your searches by using the options in the Find dialog box and by entering special characters, as follows:

Direction options →
- Use the Direction options to search backward or forward from the insertion point.

Whole Word option →
- Use the Whole Word option to find only whole-word occurrences of the Find What text. For example, find the word *men* and not the characters *men* in *mention* and *fundamental*.

Match Upper/Lowercase option →
- Use the Match Upper/Lowercase option to find only those occurrences of the Find What text with the exact capitalization specified. For example, find the initials *USA* and not the characters *usa* in *usability*. (However, the characters *USA* in *USABILITY* will be found unless you also select the Whole Word option.)

Special characters →
- Find special characters, such as tabs (enter ^t in the Find What text box), end-of-line marks (enter ^n), and paragraph symbols (enter ^p). For example, find every occurrence of a paragraph that begins with the word *Remember* by entering ^pRemember as the Find What text. Word then looks for a paragraph symbol at the end of one paragraph followed by the word *Remember* at the beginning of the next paragraph.

Wildcard characters →
- Find strings of characters when some of the characters vary or are unknown, by using ? as a "wildcard," or placeholder, in the Find What text box.

Let's work through a find procedure using a wildcard so that you can see how they operate. Suppose you regularly confuse the two words *affect* and *effect*. You can check your use of these words in the backgrounder, as follows:

1. Press Ctrl-Home to move to the beginning of the document.
2. Choose Find from the Edit menu, enter *?ffect* in the Find What text box, and press Enter to start the search. Word stops at the word *affects* in the second body-text paragraph.

3. This use of *affects* is incorrect, so click Cancel to close the dialog box, and change the *a* to *e*.
4. Press Shift-F4 to repeat the search. Word stops at the word *effects*, which is correct.
5. Press Shift-F4 again to ensure that the document contains no other instances of the Find What text.

Replacing Text

Often, you will search a document for a series of characters with the intention of replacing them. When you suspect that you will need to make the same replacement more than a couple of times, you should use the Replace command to automate the process as much as possible. As with the Find command, using the Replace command for basic substitutions is easy. We'll walk through the simplest kind of procedure first, and then we'll explain some of the possible refinements.

In the earlier section about modifying glossary entries, you changed one occurrence of *National BEAT* to *USA BEAT*, leaving two occurrences of *National BEAT* unchanged. Let's find those two occurrences of the old name and replace them with the new.

1. Press Ctrl-Home to move to the beginning of the document, and then choose the Replace command from the Edit menu. Word then displays the dialog box shown on the next page.

Stopping Find and Replace

You can stop the Find and Replace commands by pressing the Esc key. Word then scrolls the document to the place where the procedure ended. ♦

Copying find or replace text

The Find What and Replace With text boxes can hold only 255 characters. If your text has more than 255 characters, you can copy it to the Clipboard and then tell Word to use the contents of the Clipboard as the text by typing ^c in the Find What or Replace With text box. Any replacements Word makes will have the formatting of the original selection. ♦

Global replacing

To change all instances of the same word or phrase: **1.** Choose Replace. **2.** Type the Find What and Replace With text strings. **3.** Click the Replace All button. **4.** When Word announces in the status bar how many changes it made, close the dialog box. ♦

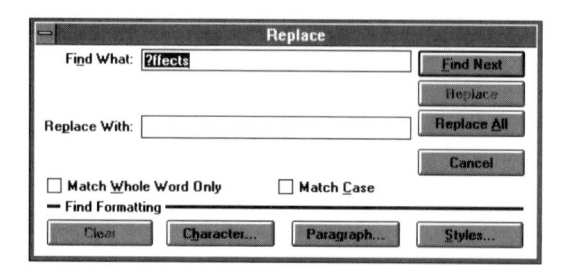

Notice that the Find What text from the previous search is in this dialog box's Find What text box.

2. Replace the Find What text by typing *National BEAT*.
3. In the Replace With text box, type *USA BEAT*.
4. Press Enter. Word highlights the first occurrence of the Find What text, and your screen looks like this:

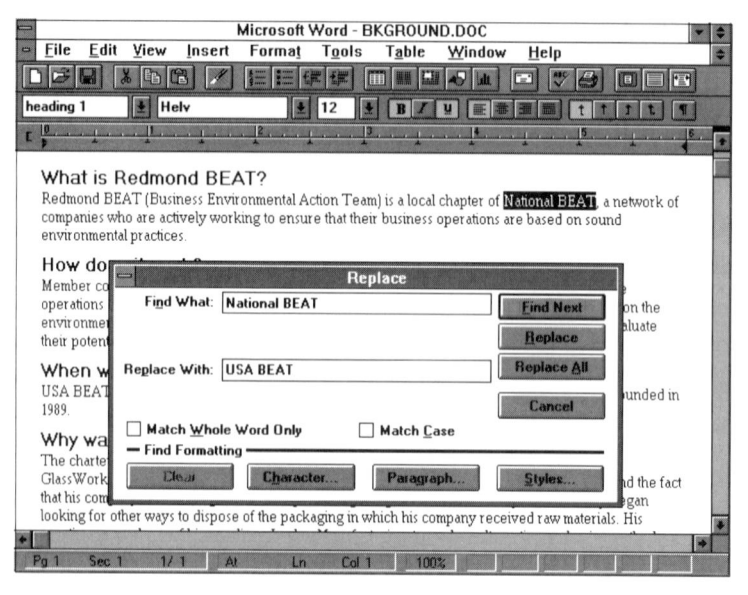

5. Click Replace. Word continues the search and highlights the second occurrence.
6. Click Replace again. Word completes the search and, when you close the dialog box, indicates in the status bar that it replaced two occurrences of the Find What text with the Replace With text.

As with the Find command, you can use the Whole Word and Match Case options and the ? wildcard to refine the replace procedure. And you can use special characters in both the Find What and Replace With text boxes. (See page 46 for more information.)

Checking Spelling

Even if you got all the way to the National Spelling Bee finals as a kid, you'll want to check the spelling of your documents before you expose them to the scrutiny of the outside world. Nothing detracts from the power of your arguments and the luster of your professional image like a typo. In the past, your readers might have overlooked the occassional misspelling. These days, running your word processor's spell-checker is so easy that readers tend to be less forgiving. The moral: Get in the habit of spell-checking all your documents, especially before printing review copies.

You can use Word's Spelling feature to check an entire document or a block of selected text. You can check against Word's built-in dictionary or against specialized dictionaries that you create.

Spell-Checking an Entire Document

As you created the backgrounder in this chapter, you deliberately included a few errors. Now its time to spell-check the document.

1. With the insertion point located at the top of the backgrounder, choose Spelling from the Tools menu. Word automatically begins spell-checking the document, starting with the word containing the insertion point. When Word finds a word that is not in its dictionary, it displays this Spelling dialog box:

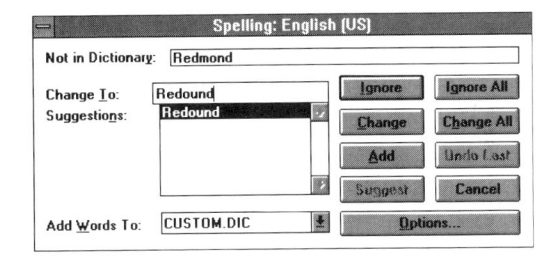

   Notice that by default Word will use the English (US) dictionary as its Main dictionary, supplemented by CUSTOM.DIC, which will be empty until you add entries to it.   *Main dictionary*

As you can see, Word didn't get very far, but stopped at the word *Redmond*. Possible substitutes appear in the Suggestions list box, with the closest match to the unrecognized word displayed in the Change To box.

2. Click the Ignore All button to tell Word that you want to leave all occurrences of this word as they are. Word continues the spell-check, stops at *environmently*, and suggests the correct spelling, *environmentally*, in the Suggestions list box and in the Change To text box.

3. Click Change to replace the unrecognized word with the suggestion. If Word's suggestion is not correct but one of the words in the Suggestions list box is the one you want, you can select that word and then click Change. If none of the suggestions is correct, you can type the correction in the Change To text box and then click Change. (You can also edit the word directly in the document without closing the dialog box.)

4. Ignore the "incorrect" words the program finds until it stops at *campaining*—another genuine misspelling. Then click Change to accept Word's suggestion, *campaigning*.

5. When Word reaches the end of the document, it closes the Spelling window and displays the message *Spell check complete* in an alert box. Click OK to close the box and return to your document.

Duplicate words	**Unconventional case**	**Case-sensitive suggestions**
If your document contains duplicate words, such as *the the*, Word stops at the words and displays them in the Spelling window. Clicking Delete deletes the duplicate word. ♦	When you choose the Spelling command, Word also stops at strange combinations of uppercase and lowercase letters. For example, Word would stumble over *NAtional* and would suggest *National* as an appropriate substitute. ♦	Word's suggestions generally have the same case as the misspelled word. For example, if the misspelling occurs at the beginning of a sentence and therefore starts with a capital letter, Word's suggestions also start with capital letters. ♦

Spell-Checking a Selection

To spell-check part of a document or even a single word, select the text or word, and then choose Spelling. Word checks the selection the same way it checks an entire document, and you use the same techniques to ignore or change any words the program does not recognize.

Creating and Using Custom Dictionaries

As you have seen, you can tell Word to remember the words it should ignore during a spell-check so that it does not stumble over them if they occur later in the document. However, when it comes to misspellings, Word has no long-term memory. The next time you use the Spelling program, it will again stop at those same words. That's where custom dictionaries come in handy. You can add names, technical terms, and other nonstandard words that you use frequently in your documents to one of these dictionaries so that Word no longer flags them every time you perform a spell-check.

Follow these steps to add a few words to CUSTOM.DIC:

1. Choose Spelling from the Tools menu to begin spell-checking the backgrounder again.
2. When Word displays *Redmond* in the Spelling window, click the Add button. Once the word is listed in an open custom dictionary, Word no longer treats it as a misspelling.   *Adding words to dictionaries*
3. Press the Esc key to halt the spell-check.

Word automatically saves the addition you have made to the user dictionary.

You don't have to store words in CUSTOM.DIC. You can create specialized user dictionaries for use with various kinds of documents. Here's how:

1. Press Ctrl-Home to move to the top of the document, and choose Spelling from the Tools menu.
2. In the Spelling dialog box, click Options to display the dialog box shown on the next page.

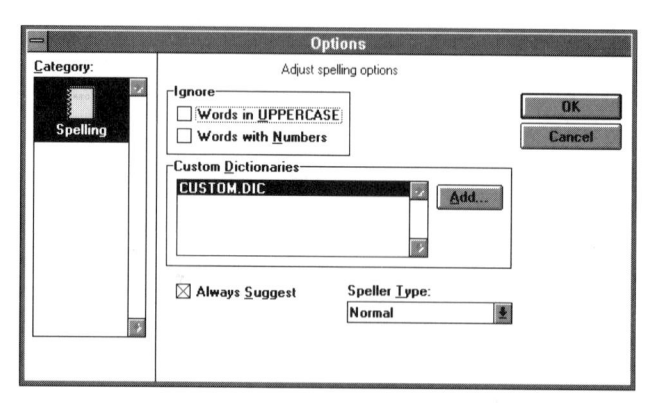

Opening a new custom dictionary

3. Click Add in the Custom Dictionaries section, type R_BEAT in the resulting dialog box, and press Enter. Notice that Word has added R_BEAT.DIC to the list of custom dictionaries.
4. Click OK to close the Options dialog box.
5. In the Spelling dialog box, press Alt-W to open the list of dictionaries, and select R_BEAT.
6. With *dumpsters* highlighted, click the Add button to add this word to the R_BEAT dictionary. Word continues the spell-check, stumbling over *Jordon* and *GlassWorks*, which you can also add to the dictionary.

You can't rely on Word's Spelling feature to identify every error in your documents. Errors of grammar, syntax, or improper word usage will pass muster in a spell-check as long as the words are spelled correctly. To catch these types of errors, you need to use Word's Grammar feature, which we discuss next.

Checking Grammar

Word's Grammar program applies common rules to your text and identifies potential problems, suggesting corrections where appropriate and providing helpful explanations if you request them. During a grammar-check, Word also spell-checks the document and accumulates statistics about the document that assess its readability.

To run the grammar-checker on BKGROUND.DOC:

1. Press Ctrl-Home to move to the top of the document, and then choose Grammar from the Tools menu. The grammar-checker highlights the paragraph under *What Is Redmond BEAT?* and suggests that part of the paragraph might be in the passive voice:

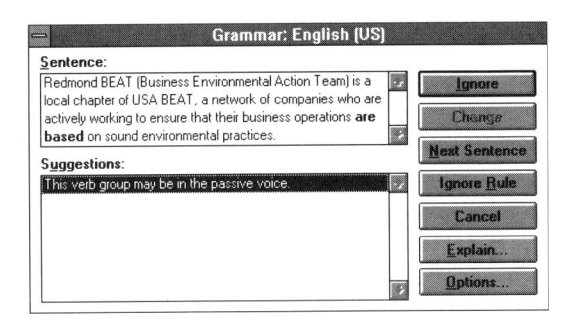

[Screenshot of Grammar: English (US) dialog box showing sentence "Redmond BEAT (Business Environmental Action Team) is a local chapter of USA BEAT, a network of companies who are actively working to ensure that their business operations are based on sound environmental practices." with suggestion "This verb group may be in the passive voice." and buttons: Ignore, Change, Next Sentence, Ignore Rule, Cancel, Explain, Options.]

2. Click Ignore Rule to tell Word not to check that rule anymore for this document. Word next highlights the sentence under *How Does It Work?* and suggests changing the obviously incorrect *there* to *their*.
3. Click Change. Click Ignore for any other potential problems, until the grammar-checker suggests changing *it's* to *its*, at which time click Change again. Then click Ignore for any other errors.
4. When Word finishes checking the document, it displays a Readability Statistics dialog box. Click OK to close it.

You can also make changes directly to your document without closing the Grammar dialog box.

As you have seen, the grammar-checker questions many elements of your document that are perfectly fine, and after checking a few documents, you might want to customize the Grammar program to match your writing style and the current document's tone. Unlike many grammar-checkers, the program that comes with Word for Windows is very flexible. If you don't want certain rules of grammar to be applied to your writing, you have the choice of turning them off. Either click the Options button in the Grammar dialog box or choose Options from the Tools menu, click the Grammar icon, and click the Customize Settings button. You can then select the rules you want to check, individually or as a set. By default, Word uses grammar rules for business writers; selecting For Casual Writing applies fewer rules, and selecting Strictly uses all the rules. To see an explanation of a rule, highlight it, and click Explain.

Specifying rules

Take the time to experiment with the grammar-checker. Fake a few errors, and see whether it catches them. The program is not infallible but running it on important documents might save you from unpleasant embarrassments.

3

Eye-Catching Documents: Creating a Flyer

Finding Files   57
   Locating the File You Need   57
   Opening a File from File Find   60
Merging One File into Another   60
More About Formatting   61
   Making Titles Stand Out   61
   Adding Borders and Shading   62
   Adding Footnotes   63
   Setting Up Multiple Columns   65
   Formatting Lists   68
Formatting with Styles   69
   Using Word's Predefined Styles   70
   Creating Custom Styles   71
     Defining Styles   71
     Modifying Styles   73
   Applying Styles   74
   Applying Styles as You Type   75
   Transferring Styles to Other Documents   77
Finishing Touches   78

Creating a search path
Page 59

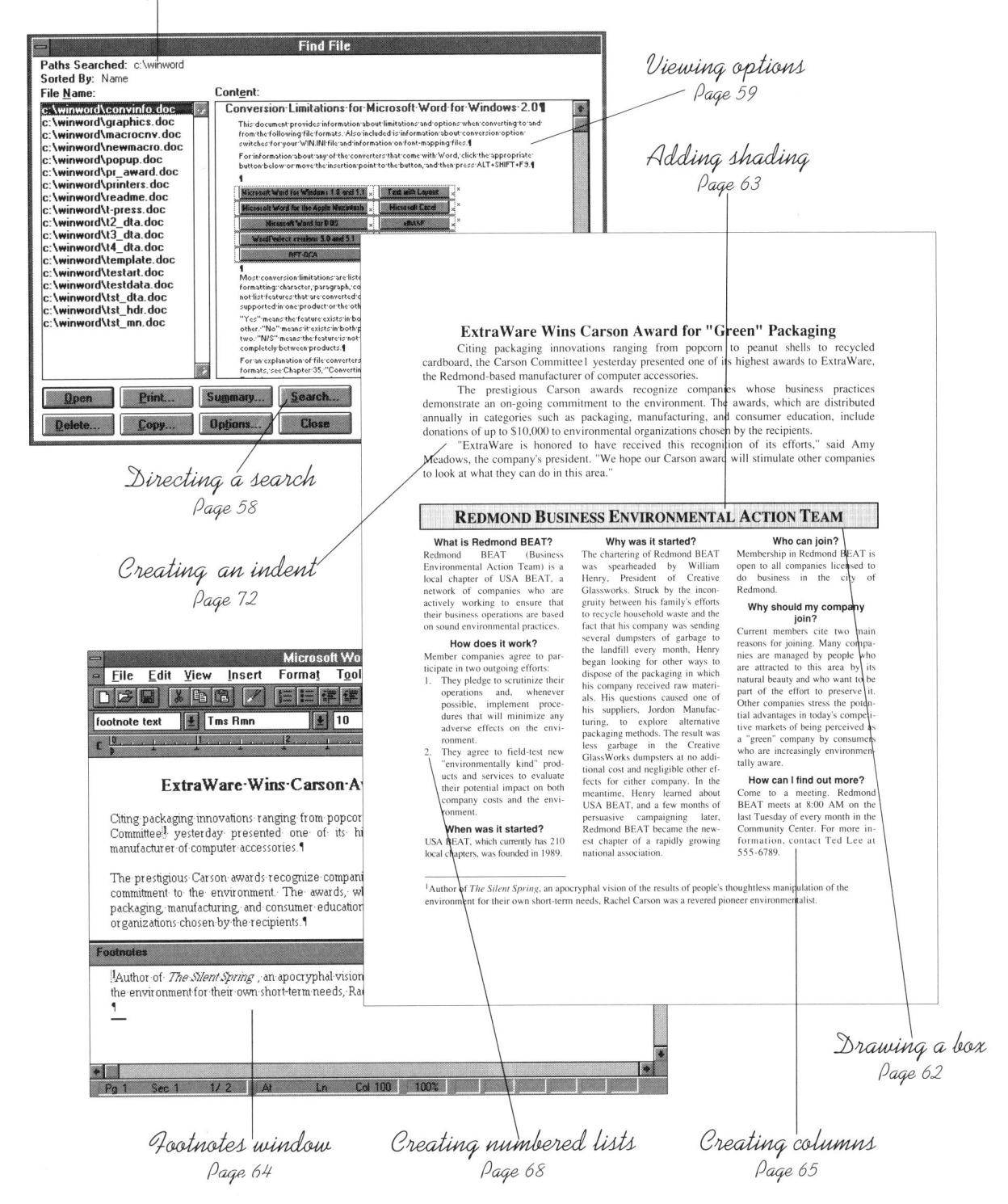

Viewing options
Page 59

Adding shading
Page 63

Directing a search
Page 58

Creating an indent
Page 72

Drawing a box
Page 62

Footnotes window
Page 64

Creating numbered lists
Page 68

Creating columns
Page 65

Everybody has their own style—that special something that sets them apart from others. For some people it is the way they dress; for others it is the way they walk, talk, hold their head, or any combination of physical, mental, and emotional attributes. Likewise, documents have style. We quickly recognize a newspaper clipping or a memo based on its formatting.

As you've seen, Word makes it easy to apply a variety of character and paragraph formats that give the different portions of your documents a distinctive style. You can apply a particular combination of formatting to a paragraph and have that combination carried on to each new paragraph you create by simply pressing Enter. When you want to switch to some other combination of formats, you can do so either by clicking buttons on the Ribbon as you did in Chapter 1 or by choosing commands from the Format menu.

A well-designed document uses formatting to provide visual cues about its structure. For example, a report might use large bold type for first-level headings and smaller bold type for second-level headings. Summary paragraphs might be indented and italic. Of course, you can work through a document applying formats to headings and summary paragraphs one by one, but Word provides an easier way. You can store custom combinations of formatting by defining the combination as a style. You can then apply that combination to a paragraph simply by selecting the style from the Style drop-down list on the Ribbon. Just as you would list the ingredients for a particular kind of cake on a card rather than try to remember the recipe each time you bake the cake, it is more efficient to store formatting combinations as styles. And because the process of creating styles is so easy, it makes sense to have a style for every combination of formats you use regularly.

In this chapter, we show you how to combine the press release from Chapter 1 and the backgrounder from Chapter 2 to create a flyer. We explore a few more formatting techniques and then show you how to turn combinations of formats into styles that you can apply with a couple of clicks of the mouse button.

Before we proceed, here's a word of warning: When it comes to formatting, use restraint. We don't want to stifle the truly creative among you—in the hands of a skilled designer, the innovative juxtaposition of different styles can produce dynamite results. However, the rest of us are just as likely to produce visual disasters. In the business world, it's better for your documents to err on the conservative side, using tried-and-true combinations and adherring to basic principles of balance and good taste, than to break new ground and risk appearing amateurish or frivolous.

Finding Files

When you saved the press release in Chapter 1 and the backgrounder in Chapter 2, you filled in Summary Info dialog boxes with information that described the files. When we first discussed the Summary Info dialog box, we explained that this extra step might save you time later if you needed to locate the files. Now you have the opportunity to put the information in these dialog boxes to use.

Locating the File You Need

Suppose you have written not two but two hundred documents, and you need to locate the Carson award press release and the Redmond BEAT backgrounder to create a flyer that will be used to attract new Redmond BEAT members. Did you call the files CARSON.DOC and REDBEAT.DOC? Or AWARD_PR.DOC and RED_BACK.DOC? And which directory did you store them in? Fortunately, with Word's Find File command you can find files without knowing their exact names and locations. Try this:

1. With Word loaded and no document open on your screen, choose Find File from the File menu. Word displays a dialog box similar to the one on the next page.

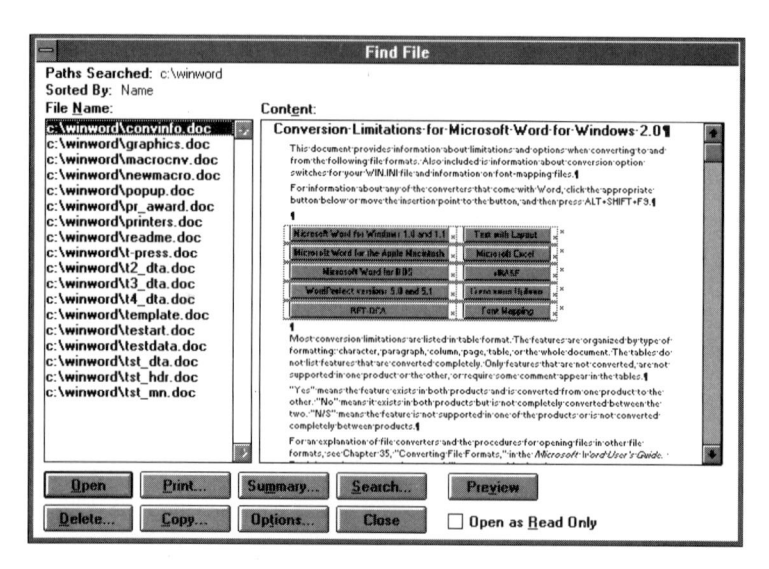

Word has already performed a search based on the settings currently in the dialog box (those used the last time the command was chosen). It has searched the paths listed at the top of the dialog box for files with the specified extension, and has listed the results in the File Name list box. If Word can read the highlighted file at the top of the list, it displays the file's contents in the Content box.

Directing a search

2. To direct a search for the file you want, click the Search button to display a Search dialog box like this one:

Here you can refine a search by specifying the extension to search for, the drives and directories to be searched, and other information. The object is to specify only as much information as is needed to find the desired files.

3. Be sure that the Type entry is Word Document (*.doc) and that the Drives entry is your hard drive. (Both

Chapter 3 Eye-Catching Documents: Creating a Flyer

entries can be selected from a list by clicking the arrow to the right of the box.)

4. In the Subject text box, type *Carson award*, and then click Start Search. Word searches the Summary Info dialog boxes of the files with the DOC extension for entries that match the criteria you have specified. It then redisplays the Find File dialog box with the names of matching files—in this case, PR_AWARD.DOC—in the File Name list box.

For this example, you want to find two files written about different subjects. Here's how to find the second file:

1. Click the Search button to redisplay the Search dialog box with your original search criteria.
2. Delete *Carson award* from the Subject text box, and enter *Redmond BEAT* in the Title text box.
3. Click the down arrow to the right of the Options box, and select Add Matches To List from the list box.
4. Reselect your drive letter from the Drives list. (Word always resets this setting to Path Only.)
5. Click Start Search. Word searches the Summary Info dialog boxes of the files with DOC extensions for entries that match the new criteria. When the Find File dialog box reappears, BKGROUND.DOC has been added to the File Name list box and appears in the Content window.

Creating a search path

If you have a general idea of where your files are, save search time by telling Word where to look. **1.** Click Edit Path in the Search dialog box. **2.** In the Edit Path dialog box, use the Drives and Directories lists to find the directories to search, and click Add to add them to the path. **3.** Click Close. The path appears in the Search dialog box's Path text box. ♦

Sorting found files

By default, Word displays files in the File Name list in alphabetical order. To list files in a different order, click Options in the Find File dialog box. You can sort by the author, the creation date, the name of the person who last saved the document, the date on which it was last saved, and the file size. ♦

Viewing options

By default, Word displays the contents of the file highlighted in the File Name list box if it is a text file. If it is a graphics file, you must click the Preview button to see the file's contents. To display information about the file, click Options. From the Options dialog box, you can choose to view the highlighted file's title, summary information, or statistics. ♦

Opening a File from File Find

Having located the files, you can open, print, delete, or copy them from the Find File dialog box. You can perform any of these operations on several files at once by selecting them in the Find File list. You can also change their summary information. Here, we'll show you how to open one of the files. Follow these steps:

1. Be sure that BKGROUND.DOC is selected in the Find File dialog box.
2. Click the Open button. Word closes the Find File dialog box and opens BKGROUND.DOC.

Merging One File into Another

To create the membership flyer, we want to use both the backgrounder and the press release. With Word, merging documents is easy. BKGROUND.DOC is currently open on your screen, so let's merge in PR_AWARD.DOC and then get to work on formatting the flyer.

1. To safeguard the original backgrounder file, choose Save As from the File menu, and change the name of the version now on your screen to FLYER.DOC.
2. Press Ctrl-Home to be sure that the insertion point is at the top of the backgrounder document.
3. Choose File from the Insert menu. Word displays this dialog box:

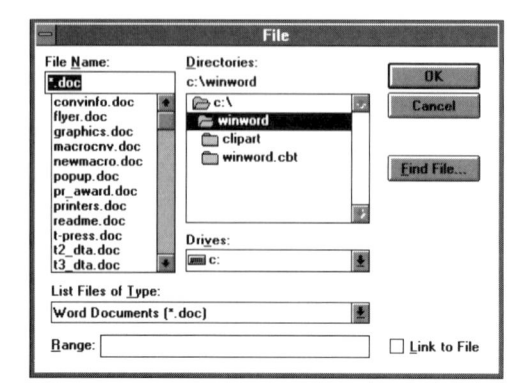

As you can see, this dialog box is similar to the Open dialog box. If the file you want is not listed in the File Name list box, you can locate the file by clicking folder icons in the Directories list box to change the displayed

directory, or by clicking the Find File button to access the Find File dialog box.
4. Select PR_AWARD.DOC from the File Name list box, and click OK.
5. Press Ctrl-Home to move to the top of the document, and select and delete the *PRESS RELEASE* heading.
6. Select and delete *November 23, 1991. Redmond, Washington* and the following space.
7. Select and then delete the three right-aligned contact-information lines and the paragraph symbol at the bottom of the press release.
8. Click the Save button on the Toolbar to save the combined document.

More About Formatting

In Chapter 1, we covered some of the simple ways you can dress up a document using the character-formatting and paragraph-formatting buttons on the Ribbon. Let's now look at some more sophisticated formatting techniques—a few implemented with buttons and a few implemented using commands on the Format menu.

Making Titles Stand Out

As you know, you apply character formatting when you want to change the appearance of individual characters. Here we'll focus on the titles of the two "articles" in the new flyer, and we'll use options on the Ribbon as well as in the Character dialog box to control the way the titles look. Let's get started.

1. Move to the top of the document, select the title of the press release, and click the Italic button to turn off italic formatting.
2. Change the font to Tms Roman, and change the size to 16 points.
3. Now select *Redmond Business Environmental Action Team*, the title of the backgrounder. Click the Center button on the Ribbon to center the title, click the Underline button to turn off underlining, and then change the font to Tms Rmn and the size to 18 points.
4. Choose Character from the Format menu. Word displays the dialog box shown on the next page.

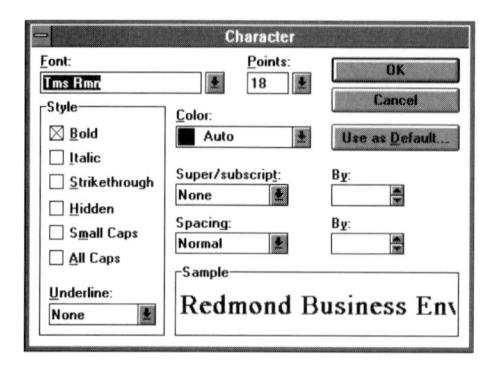

As you can see, the dialog box reflects the Font and Size settings you just made. It also provides several other formatting options.

Small Caps →
5. Click Small Caps in the Style section to format the title in small capital letters with large initial capital letters.
6. Click OK to close the dialog box and implement your selections.

If you want, you can experiment with some of the other options in the Character dialog box before moving on.

Adding Borders and Shading

To add emphasis to particular paragraphs, you can draw lines above and below or to the left and right of them, or you can surround the paragraphs with different styles of boxes. Let's box the backgrounder title:

1. With the backgrounder title still selected, choose Border from the Format menu to display this dialog box:

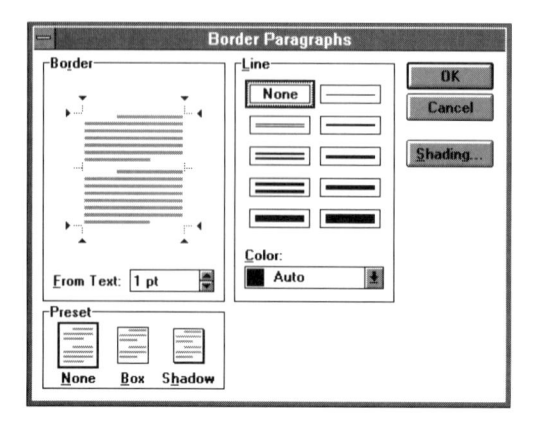

Drawing a box →
2. In the Preset section, select Box. Word draws a box around the diagram in the Border section on the left side of the dialog box.

3. In the Line section, select the second single line.
4. Click the Shading button to display this dialog box:

Adding shading

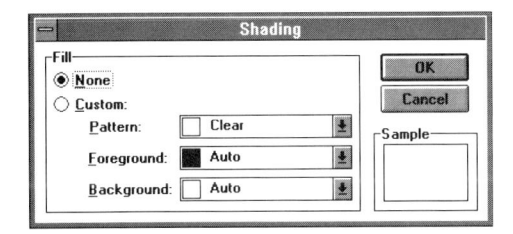

5. Click Custom, select 25% from the Pattern drop-down list box, and click OK twice. Click anywhere to remove the highlighting so that you can see these results:

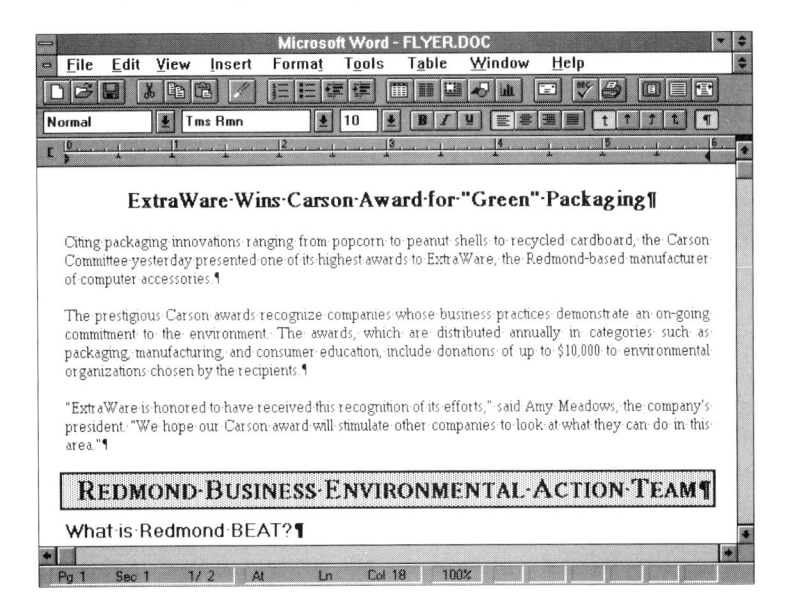

Again, you might want to experiment with the other possible combinations in the Border Paragraphs dialog box before we move on to talk about creating footnotes.

Adding Footnotes

Footnotes are used to document sources and give tangential information when its inclusion in the body of the text would detract from the main thrust of a discussion. We are including a brief overview of footnotes in this chapter because they entail special formatting. Their reference marks in the text are usually superscripted, and the footnotes themselves are usually gathered at the bottom of the page or at the end of the document. Fortunately, Word takes care of a lot of the necessary formatting for you.

As an example, suppose you want to mention the origin of the Carson Committee in the flyer, but you can't think of a graceful way of including it in the press release. The simple solution is to put the information in a footnote. Here's how:

1. Click an insertion point after the word *Committee* in the first paragraph of the press release, and choose Footnote from the Insert menu. Word displays this dialog box:

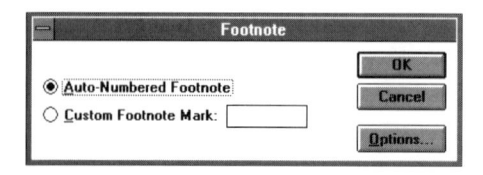

Automatic numbers

By default, Word will automatically number footnotes.

2. Click OK. Word inserts a superscripted 1 after the word *Committee* and opens a Footnotes window at the bottom of your screen, ready for you to type the footnote.

Footnotes window

3. Type the following, formatting *The Silent Spring* in italics as shown:

Author of *The Silent Spring*, an apocryphal vision of the results of people's thoughtless manipulation of the environment for their own short-term needs, Rachel Carson was a revered pioneer environmentalist.

Here's how your screen looks now:

Deleting footnotes	Footnote placement	Numbering options
To delete a footnote: **1.** Highlight the footnote reference mark in the text. **2.** Press Del. Word then deletes all the footnote text. If you are using automatically generated numbers, Word also renumbers all subsequent footnotes. ♦	By default, Word places footnotes at the bottom of the page. You can have Word place them at the end of a section, at the end of the entire document, or after the last line of text on a page. (This last option is useful for pages that are less than full length.) Click Options in the Footnote dialog box to access these options. ♦	Use the numbering options in the Footnote Options dialog box to start footnote numbering at a number other than 1. Select the Restart Each Section option to have footnote numbering start at 1 for each new document section. ♦

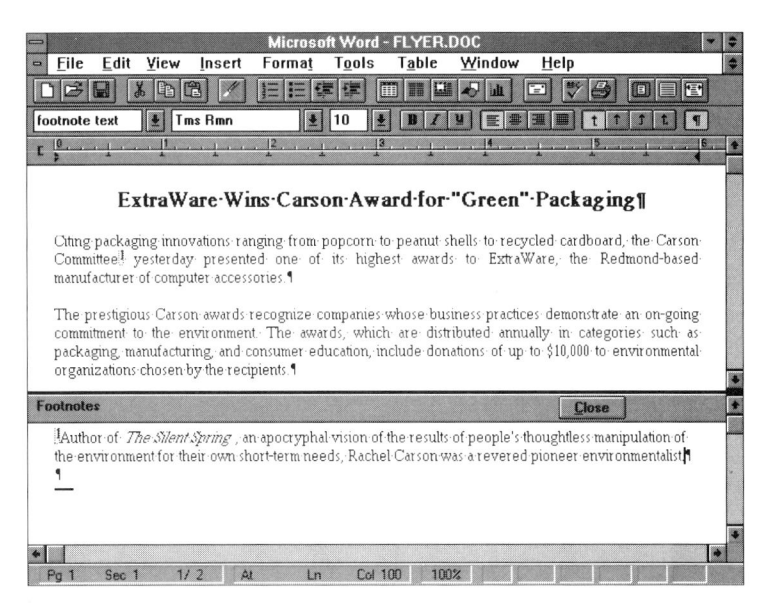

[Screenshot of Microsoft Word - FLYER.DOC showing the document with footnotes window open]

4. Click the Close button to close the Footnotes window.
5. Choose Print Preview from the File menu so that you can see exactly how Word will position the footnote when you print the document. Then click the Cancel button to return to your document.

Previewing footnotes

That's the simple way to create footnotes. You can also assign your own reference marks to footnotes. But why complicate things? Our advice is to let Word keep track of footnotes with automatically numbered reference marks so that you can concentrate on more important matters.

Setting Up Multiple Columns

Newsletters and flyers often feature multicolumn layouts like those of magazines and newspapers. These layouts give you more flexibility when it comes to the placement of elements on the page and they are often visually more interesting than single-column layouts.

With Word, setting up multiple columns for an entire document couldn't be easier. You simply click the Columns button on the Toolbar and select the number of columns you want. When you want only part of your document to have a multicolumn layout, you simply select that part of the document and choose Columns from the Format menu. You then tell Word to set up the selected text in columns in a separate section so that it knows where to stop formatting your text in one column, where to start formatting it in multiple columns, and where to return to one column.

Creating columns

Suppose we want the press-release text to be one column, the backgrounder text to be three columns, and any text we might add after the backgrounder to be one column. To create this layout, follow these steps:

1. Press Ctrl-End to move to the end of the document, and, if necessary, press Enter to create an empty paragraph below the backgrounder.
2. Click an insertion point at the end of the last backgrounder paragraph, scroll until you can see the *What is Redmond BEAT?* heading, hold down the Shift key, and click at the beginning of the heading. The entire backgrounder except the title is now selected, and the empty paragraph at the end of the document is not selected. (If you include the empty paragraph in the selection, the footnote you created earlier will also be affected by the three-column format.)
3. Choose Columns from the Format menu to display this dialog box:

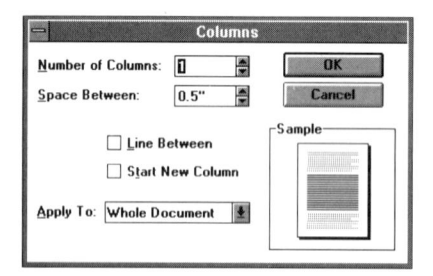

Using the Columns button

To use the Columns button to create a multicolumn format (or change a multicolumn layout to one column): **1.** Click the Columns button. **2.** Drag through the number of columns you want. That's it! The icon expands to six columns if you drag past the right edge. If you want more than six columns, you must use the Columns command on the Format menu. ♦

Inserting column breaks

Word automatically breaks columns of text at the bottom of the page. Here's how to force a column to break before the bottom of the page: **1.** Place the insertion point where you would like the break to occur. **2.** Choose Break from the Insert menu. **3.** Specify Column Break in the Break dialog box. **4.** Click OK. Use Page Layout view to see the effects. ♦

Inserting section breaks

Word applies column formats to an entire section. To insert section breaks so that you can vary the number of columns in different parts of a document: **1.** Choose Break from the Insert menu. **2.** Click an option in the Section Break area. **3.** Click OK. Word inserts a double dotted section break above the insertion point, which moves down into the next section. ♦

4. Change the Number Of Columns to 3 and the entry in the Space Between text box to .25".
5. Select the Selected Text option from the Apply To drop-down list box, and click OK. Word puts a section break (a double dotted line) at the beginning of the selected text and another at the end, and reformats the text so that it snakes across the page in three columns. However, because you are in Normal view, you see only one skinny column on the left side of your screen.
6. Choose Print Preview from the File menu to see the effects of the three-column layout.

Viewing columns in Print Preview

As you can see, Word has bumped the entire backgrounder text to the second page. Why? Because of the footnote. For some reason, Word cannot handle continuous sections *and* put footnotes at the bottom of the page. The best way around this layout problem is to specify that the footnotes appear at the end of the document. Here's how:

1. Choose Footnote from the Insert menu to display the Footnote dialog box, and then click Options. Word displays this dialog box:

Relocating footnotes

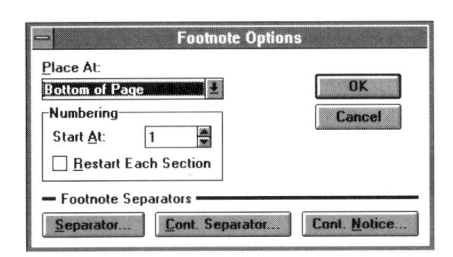

2. Pull down the Place At list box, select End Of Document, and click OK to implement your change. Then click the Close button to close the Footnotes window.
3. We'll take this opportunity to introduce Page Layout view. This view is a cross between Print Preview and Normal view—it allows you to both see the layout of your document and edit and format the text. Choose Page Layout from the View menu, and scroll until the *REDMOND BUSINESS ENVIRONMENTAL ACTION TEAM* title is at the top of your screen, which now looks like the one shown on the next page.

Page Layout view

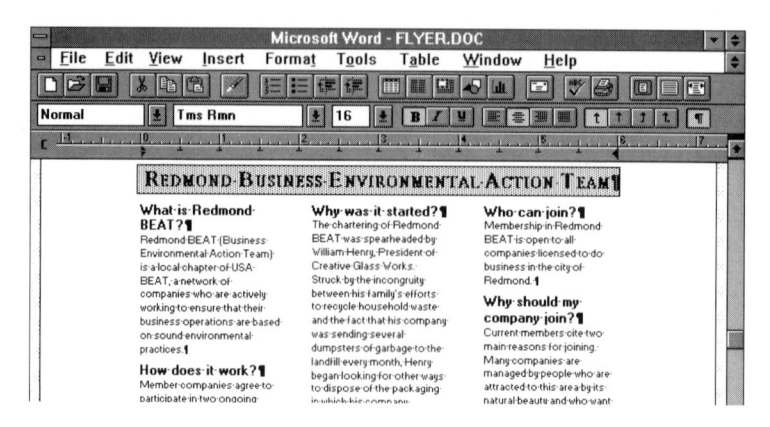

Formatting Lists

The second paragraph of the backgrounder contains two numbered items that would stand out better if they were set up in a list format. Word has two built-in list formats: one for numbered lists and one for bulleted lists. Here's how you implement the numbered-list format (the bulleted-list format works the same way):

1. Click an insertion point in front of the *T* of the first *They* in the second paragraph, press Backspace four times to delete 1. and its surrounding spaces, and then press Enter.
2. Click an insertion point in front of the *T* of the second *They*, press Backspace four times to delete 2. and its surrounding spaces, and press Enter. The formerly numbered items now appear in their own paragraphs.
3. Select the new paragraphs, and then click the Numbered List button on the Toolbar. Here's the result:

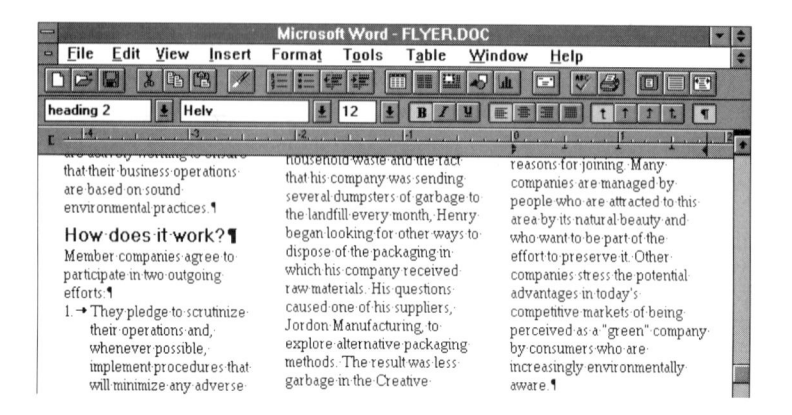

Creating numbered lists

Word has renumbered the two paragraphs and given them a hanging-indent format.

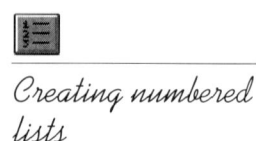

Like other elements in the document, the numbered list could do with some fine-tuning. Don't worry about this level of formatting for now. We will come back to these elements later, after we have made a few more adjustments.

Formatting with Styles

Every paragraph has a style. By default, Word applies the Normal style to the paragraphs you write, making the characters 10-point Tms Rmn and the paragraphs single spaced and aligned with the left margin. In Chapter 2, when you created an outline for the backgrounder, Word automatically applied the *heading 1* and *heading 2* styles to the headings you entered. Those styles are active in the backgrounder you have included in the flyer, so try this:

Normal style

1. Click the Normal View button, scroll up to the shaded backgrounder title, and click an insertion point in it. Notice that the Style box on the Ribbon shows that the *heading 1* style is applied to this paragraph.
2. Press the Down Arrow key several times, noting how the Style box changes to reflect the style of the paragraph that contains the insertion point.
3. Choose Options from the bottom of the Tools menu, select the View category if it isn't already selected, and enter *0.6"* in the Style Area Width text box. Click OK. Your screen then looks something like this one:

Opening the style area

As you can see, Word has opened a style area along the left edge of the screen, pushing your text to the right. The style applied to each paragraph appears in the style area. This view of your document allows you to see at a glance which styles are controlling the formatting of this document.

Closing the style area

4. Get rid of the style area by redisplaying the Options dialog box, resetting the Style Area Width to 0, and clicking OK.

Using Word's Predefined Styles

When you created the backgrounder outline in Chapter 2, designating a paragraph as a heading automatically applied a *heading* style to that paragraph. As you know, Word comes with nine predefined *heading* styles. Word also has predefined styles for a number of other common document elements, such as index entries, footnotes, and headers and footers.

Adding predefined styles

If you create a new document by choosing New from the File menu and immediately pull down the Style list by clicking the arrow to the right of the Style box, you'll see that the list of available styles includes only *heading 1*, *heading 2*, *heading 3*, and Normal. Word does not list the other predefined styles unless the current document contains the corresponding elements. If you insert one of these elements into the document, Word both applies the style to the

---

Closing with the mouse

To use the mouse to close the style area: **1.** Point to the line at the area's right edge. **2.** When the pointer changes to a double line with left- and right-pointing arrows, drag the line to the left edge of your screen. The style area disappears, and your text resumes its normal position on the screen. ♦

All or nothing

You apply styles to entire paragraphs. If you include character formatting as part of a style, that formatting becomes the base format for the entire paragraph. You cannot use styles to apply combinations of font, size, and other formats to selected characters within a paragraph without applying them to the entire paragraph. ♦

Adding styles to templates

To add a style to the template on which the new document is based, choose Style from the Format menu, select Define, click the Add To Template option, and click OK. (See page 105 for more information about templates.) ♦

element and adds the style name to the drop-down list. Check this out:

1. With the insertion point in a Normal-style paragraph, click the arrow to the right of the Style box. This list box drops down:

Displaying the Style list

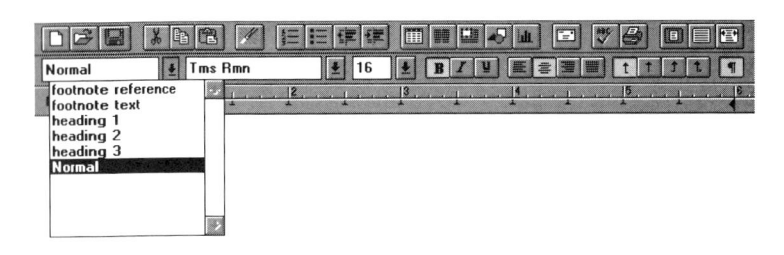

As you can see, Word has added the *footnote reference* and *footnote text* styles to the list for this document, because you inserted a footnote in the press release earlier in the chapter.

➤ Press Esc to close the list without making any changes.

When Word applies one of its predefined styles to an element, it uses the formatting that has been predefined for that element. Once the style is available on the Style list, you can manually apply the style to other paragraphs. You can also redefine the style to suit the document you are creating. We tell you how to apply styles on page 74 and how to modify styles on page 73.

Creating Custom Styles

Although Word does a good job of anticipating the document elements for which you will need styles, you will undoubtedly want to come up with styles of your own. You create custom styles by formatting a paragraph the way you want it and then defining that combination of formats as a style. After a style is defined, you can modify it and use it as the basis for creating new styles.

Defining Styles The paragraphs of the press release currently have open spacing and no first-line indent. To demonstrate the process of defining a style, let's create a style that closes up the paragraphs, indents their first lines to distinguish one paragraph from another, and makes the size of the characters slightly larger.

1. Move to the top of the document, and place the insertion point anywhere in the first text paragraph.
2. Choose Paragraph from the Format menu to display this dialog box:

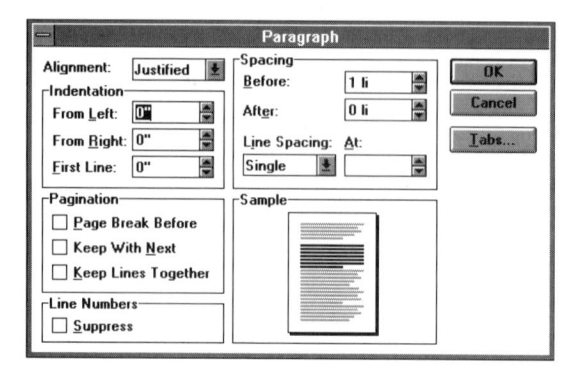

Creating an indent

3. In the Indentation section, drag through 0" in the First Line box, and type *.5*. (You don't have to type the ".)
4. In the Spacing section, drag through 1 li in the Before box, and type *0*. (Again, you don't have to type *li*.)
5. Pause for a moment to notice the effect of these new settings on the sample in the bottom-right corner of the dialog box, and then click OK.
6. With the pointer in the selection bar, double-click the mouse button to select the entire paragraph. Then select 12 from the Size box on the Ribbon.

Next, you need to define this particular combination of formatting as a style. Here goes:

1. Press Ctrl-S. Word highlights the Style bar.

Naming a style

2. Type *para indent* (for *indented paragraph*), the name you want to assign to this style. Then press Enter. Word creates the style, adds the style name to the Style list, and displays *para indent* in the Style box to indicate that it is the style applied to the current paragraph.

Now let's turn our attention to the paragraphs of the backgrounder part of the flyer. You want to justify these paragraphs, but you don't want them to have a first-line indent. Follow these steps:

1. Click an insertion point in the first text paragraph of the backgrounder, and then choose the Paragraph command from the Format menu.

2. Pull down the Alignment list box in the top-left corner of the Paragraph dialog box, and select Justified. (This is the equivalent of clicking the Justify button on the Ribbon.) Then click OK.
3. Press Ctrl-S, type *para nonindent* as this style's name, and press Enter.

That's it! You now have two custom styles available on the Styles list. Defining styles is that easy. Let's look at how you modify styles—an equally simple process.

Modifying Styles Suppose you want to globally change the formatting produced by the *heading 2* style. Try this:

1. Select the entire *What Is Redmond BEAT?* heading. Click the Center button on the Ribbon, and then select 10 from the Size drop-down list box.
2. Now redefine the style based on the new formatting combination by selecting *heading 2* from the Style drop-down list box. (Select it again, even though it is already selected.) Word displays this dialog box:

Redefining a style

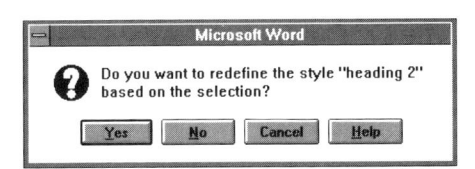

If you click Yes, Word modifies the existing style. If you click No, Word applies the selected style to the

---

Which style?	Style shortcuts	Overriding styles
If the Ribbon is not turned on, pressing Ctrl-S causes the words *Which style?* to appear in the status bar. Simply type the name you want to assign to the style, and press Enter. ♦	To apply a style from the keyboard, press Ctrl-S, type the name of the style, and press Enter. If you can't remember the name, press Ctrl-S-S to display the Styles dialog box, select the desired style, and then press Enter. To return a paragraph to Normal style, click an insertion point within the paragraph, and press Alt-Shift-5 (numeric keypad). ♦	When you apply the *para indent* style to the press release's first paragraph, Word reformats the footnote reference mark. To reformat the reference mark: **1.** Highlight it. **2.** Choose Character from the Format menu. **3.** Choose Superscript from the Super/Subscript drop-down list box and 8 from the Points drop-down list box. **4.** Click OK. ♦

paragraph, returning the paragraph to its condition before you made changes to the formatting. Clicking Cancel closes the dialog box, leaving your formatting changes intact without redefining the style.

3. Click Yes to redefine the style. Now scroll down through the backgrounder text, noticing that every second-level heading has instantly changed to 10 points with center alignment.

You can also modify a style and then store the new formatting combination with a different name so that the original style is preserved.

Applying Styles

So far, the *para indent* style is applied only to the paragraph you used when creating the style. Let's apply this style to the next two paragraphs. You can apply the same style to more than one consecutive paragraph by selecting text from all the paragraphs and then selecting the style you want. Try this:

1. With the pointer in the selection bar, hold down the mouse button, and select the last line of the second text paragraph and the first line of the third text paragraph.
2. Click the arrow to the right of the Style box to display the Style list, and select the *para indent* style. Word changes both paragraphs from Normal style to *para indent* style. Click anywhere to remove the highlighting. Your document now looks like this:

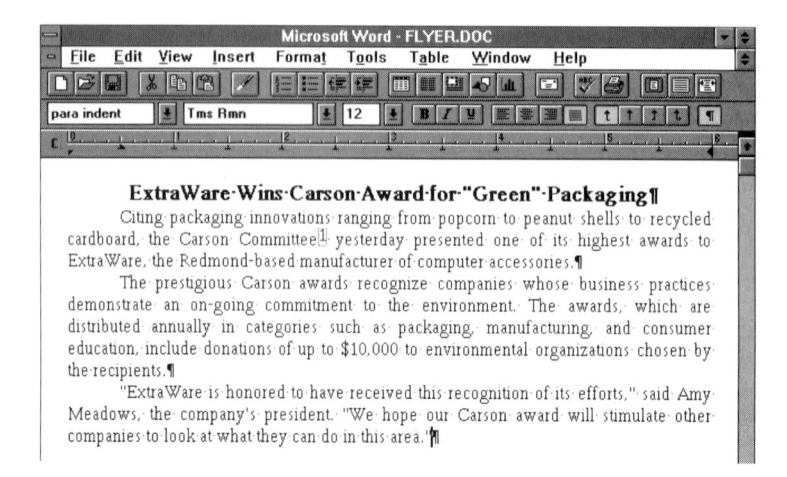

Now try a different procedure to apply the *para nonindent* style to the paragraphs of the backgrounder:

1. Click in the second text paragraph of the backgrounder (which has the Normal style), and apply the *para nonindent* style from the Style box.
2. Click in the next text paragraph (skip the numbered list and the heading), and press F4 to repeat the previous command.
3. Repeat step 2 for all remaining text paragraphs.

Don't worry that the new style messes up the numbered-list formatting. We'll take care of that in a moment.

Applying Styles as You Type

Generally, paragraphs "inherit" the style of the paragraph from which they are created. To see how this works, follow these steps:

Inheriting styles

1. Open up the style area by choosing Options from the Tools menu, setting the Style Area Width option to 0.6, and clicking OK.
2. Click an insertion point at the end of the third press-release paragraph, and press Enter to insert a new paragraph. Notice that the new paragraph has the same *para indent* style as the preceding paragraph.
3. Select the *heading 2* style from the Style drop-down list box, and type a few characters. Word formats the characters with the *heading 2* style as you type them.

Searching for styles

To search for paragraphs to which you have assigned a particular style: **1.** Choose Find from the Edit menu. **2.** Click the Styles button, select the style you want to find, and click OK. **3.** Click Find Next in the Find dialog box. Word highlights the next paragraph formatted with that style. ♦

Replacing styles

You can use the Edit menu's Replace command to globally change a particular applied style. For example, to change the *para indent* style to the *para nonindent* style: **1.** Choose Replace from the Edit menu. **2.** Click Styles, select *para indent*, and click OK. **3.** Select the Replace With text box, click Styles, select *para nonindent*, and click OK. **4.** Click either Replace or Replace All, depending on whether you want Word to pause so that you can confirm the replacement of the specified style. ♦

Style sequences

If styles occur in a set sequence, you can override the style inheritance rule. For example, if second-level headings are always followed by Normal paragraphs, you can specify that pressing Enter at the end of a second-level heading will initiate a Normal-style paragraph instead of another second-level paragraph. Word has already set up this sequence for its predefined *heading* styles. Try this:

1. Press Enter at the end of the second-level heading you just created. Notice that the new paragraph has the Normal style, not the *heading 2* style. Let's see how this relationship is established.
2. Without moving the insertion point, choose Style from the Format menu.
3. When Word displays the Style dialog box, click Define to expand the dialog box as shown here:

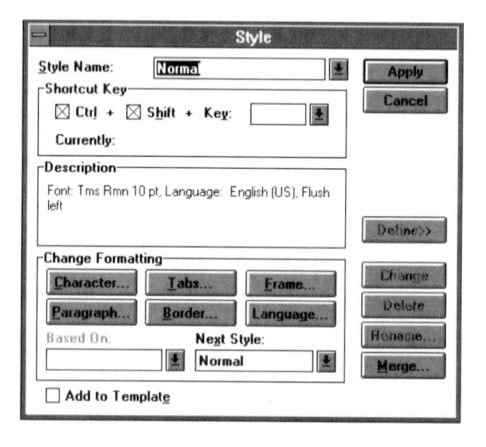

The Next Style box

The Next Style box at the bottom of the dialog box specifies the style that will be applied to the next paragraph you create. As you can see, the next paragraph you create by pressing Enter will inherit the Normal style of this paragraph.

4. Click Cancel to close the dialog box.
5. Now click an insertion point in the preceding second-level heading, choose Style from the Format menu, and again click Define. As you can see, the Next Style box specifies that instead of inheriting the style of the current *heading 2* paragraph, the next paragraph you create by pressing Enter will have the Normal style.
6. Click Cancel to close the dialog box, delete the demonstration heading and the blank paragraph above the

backgrounder title, and close the style area by resetting Style Area Width in the Options dialog box to 0.

Transferring Styles to Other Documents

Once you have created a style for use in one document, you don't have to recreate it for use in others. You can simply copy the style to the new document. Try this:

1. Click the New button on the Toolbar to create a new blank document, and then pull down its Style list box, which shows the default *heading 1*, *heading 2*, *heading 3*, and Normal styles.
2. Choose FLYER.DOC from the Window menu to redisplay the flyer, click an insertion point at the end of the third press-release paragraph, and press Enter.
3. Select the blank paragraph, which is formatted with the *para indent* style, by clicking in the selection bar. Then click the Cut button to remove the paragraph mark and store it on the Clipboard.

    Copying a style

4. Choose the blank document from the Window menu, and click the Paste button to insert the paragraph mark from the Clipboard.
5. Now pull down the Style list box. Pasting a paragraph mark formatted with the *para indent* style has added that style to the list, as you can see here:

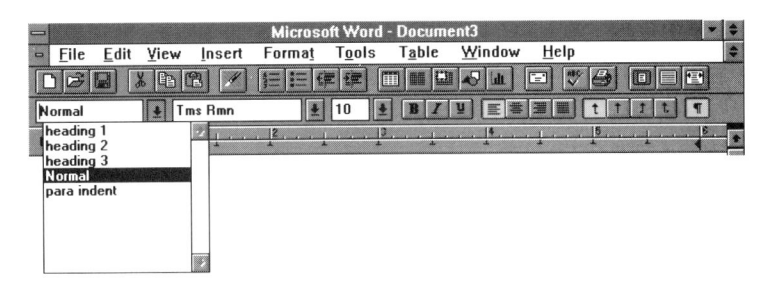

6. Close the new document without saving it.

This discussion of styles has been necessarily brief, but you now know enough to begin using styles effectively. The most important advice we can give you regarding styles is: Use them. Within a few hours, they will be second nature, and you will wonder how you ever got along without them.

Finishing Touches

As you probably realize, we are not quite finished with the flyer. The basic formatting is in place, but it needs one or two little touches to make it look more professional. First, let's adjust the numbered list:

Adjusting indents

1. Select the two numbered items, and click the Numbered List button on the Toolbar. Word reapplies the hanging-indent format.
2. The space between the numbers and their text is a little too spacey for the skinny column, so with the two paragraphs still selected, choose Paragraph from the Format menu. Word displays the dialog box shown earlier on page 72.
3. Change the From Left setting to .25 and the First Line setting to –.25, and click OK. Word closes up the space. Notice that the items retain their applied style, even though you have added additional formatting.

Now let's adjust the left and right margins to widen the text column:

Adjusting margins

1. Press Ctrl-Home, and choose Page Setup from the Format menu. Word displays this dialog box:

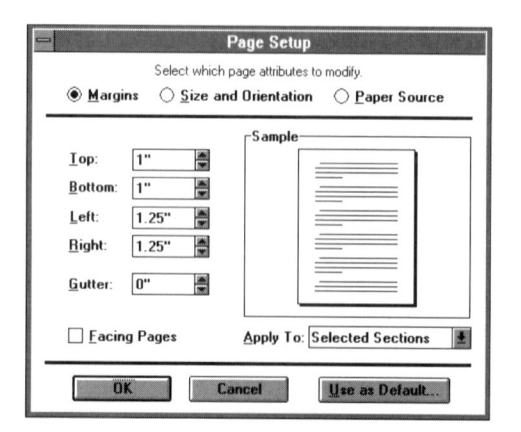

The settings in this dialog box control the basic layout of all the pages in this document. They override any corresponding settings you might have made in the dialog box displayed when you chose Print Setup from the File menu (see page 23). Because the Margins button is selected at the top of the dialog box, the options displayed pertain to your documents margins.

2. Change the settings in both the Left and Right text boxes to 1, select Whole Document from the Apply To drop-down list box, and click OK. Word adjusts the text to fit within these new margins.

The overall affect of making the margins narrower is to shorten the flyer. Let's add some space around the two titles to make them stand out more:

1. With the insertion point in the press-release title, choose Paragraph from the Format menu, set the Before option to 2, and click OK. *Adding space before*
2. Move the insertion point to the backgrounder title, and press F4 to repeat the formatting.

With all that tweaking out of the way, you have one last procedure to go through: hyphenating the document. By default, Word does not hyphenate your text, but by hyphenating some words you can really improve the looks of the justified skinny columns of the backgrounder. Here's how:

1. Press Ctrl-Home to move to the top of the document. (You may as well hyphenate the press-release text, too.) Then choose Hyphenation from the Tools menu to display this dialog box: *Hyphenating text*

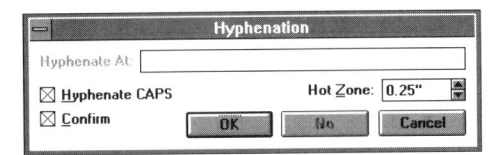

2. Click the Hyphenate CAPS option to deselect it (you don't want to hyphenate BEAT, for example), and also deselect the Confirm option to have Word hyphenate automatically. Then click OK. Word switches to Page Layout view while it hyphenates the document. *Hyphenation options*
3. When Word displays the message *Hyphenation is complete*, click OK. You are returned to your document in Normal view.

You might want to scroll through the flyer, noticing the effects of hyphenation. A lot of the big spaces between words have disappeared, and the flyer now looks much more attractive. Save the finished document, and then print it. Your flyer should look like the one at the beginning of the chapter.

4

Graphic Impact: Graphics, Tables, Charts, and Spreadsheets

Importing Word's Graphics   82
   Changing the Graphic's Size   84
Creating Tables   87
   Rearranging the Table   89
   Changing Column Width   89
   Inserting Rows   91
   Joining Cells   91
   Formatting Tables   92
Creating Charts   94
Importing Spreadsheets   97

Ready-made graphics
Page 82

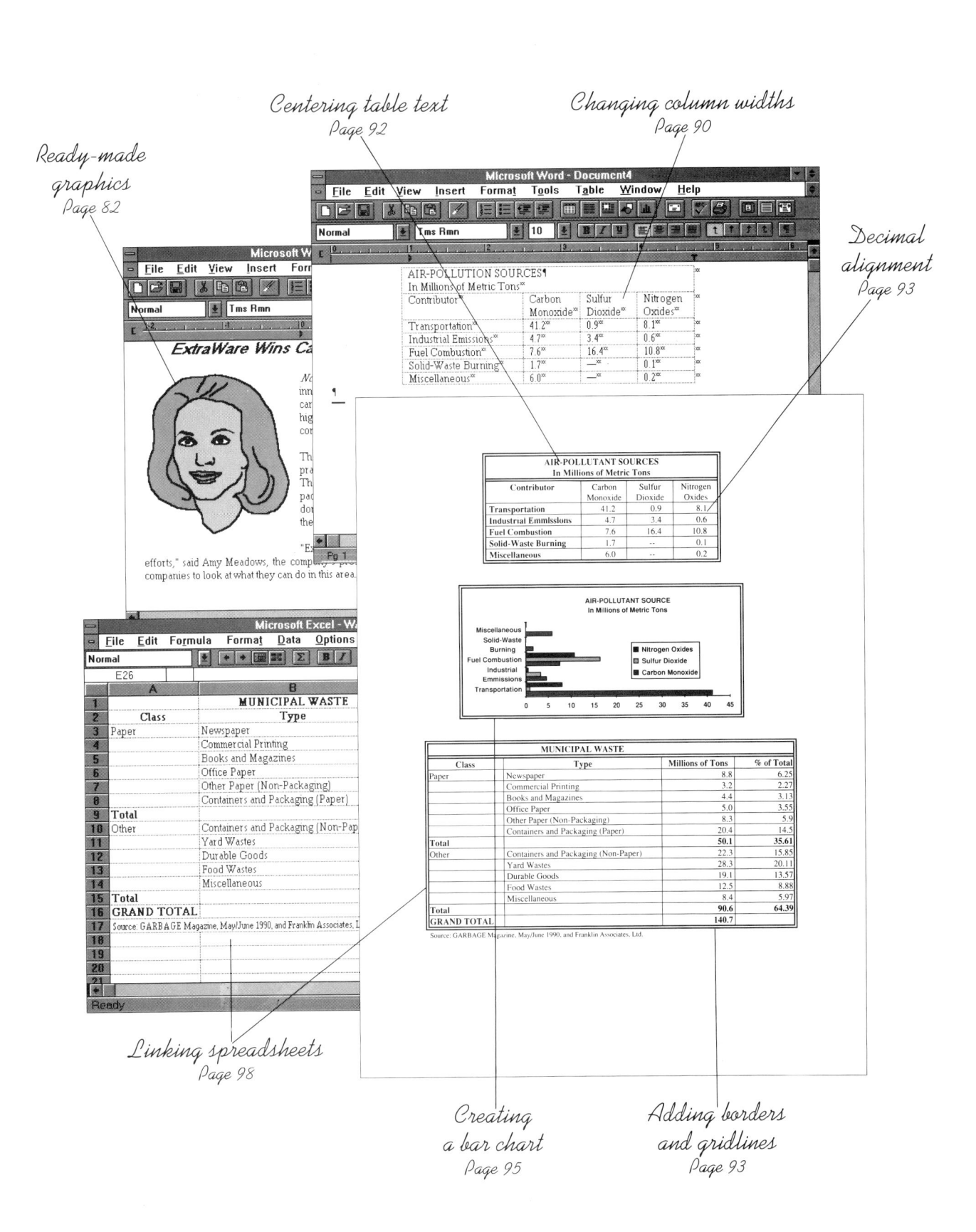

Centering table text
Page 92

Changing column widths
Page 90

Decimal alignment
Page 93

Linking spreadsheets
Page 98

Creating a bar chart
Page 95

Adding borders and gridlines
Page 93

While following the examples in the preceding chapters, you've learned a lot about Word's formatting capabilities and how to combine formats to create professional-looking documents. In this chapter, we show you a few more tricks for those times when your documents need a little more pizzazz. First we demonstrate how easily you can incorporate graphics into your Word documents. Then we cover how to create tables and charts to present facts and figures. If you've already set up your information in a spreadsheet program and don't relish the thought of having to recreate it in Word, you'll be pleased to know that you can import spreadsheet data directly into a Word table.

Importing Word's Graphics

In Chapter 3, you merged a copy of the press release you created earlier in Chapter 1 with a copy of the backgrounder you created in Chapter 2. The copies were separate text files that, after the merge, became part of the same document. In a similar way, you can merge separate graphics and text files.

Ready-made graphics

The Word for Windows software package includes a number of ready-made graphics files that are suitable for many different types of documents. We'll use one of these files (WOMAN.WMF) and the press release from Chapter 1 to demonstrate how easy it is to import graphics into Word. To follow along, the graphics files, which have WMF extensions, must have been installed. (They are probably in the C:\WINWORD\CLIPART directory on your hard disk.) If they haven't been installed, run the Word for Windows installation program to install them.

As a simple demonstration, let's add a graphic to the left of the text paragraphs of the press release. If you simply insert the graphic in a document, the text will be bumped below the graphic, instead of wrapping beside it. To position the graphic and text side-by-side, you need to create a frame in which to insert the graphic. With Word for Windows loaded and the press-release document (PR_AWARD.DOC) displayed on your screen, follow these steps to create the frame:

Chapter 4 Graphic Impact: Graphics, Tables, Charts, and Spreadsheets

1. So that you will be able to see and manipulate the graphic and its frame, choose the Page Layout command from the View menu.
2. Choose the Frame command from the Insert menu. The pointer changes to a cross hair.
3. Position the cross-hair pointer next to the word *November* at the beginning of the press release's first paragraph. Then hold down the mouse button, and keeping an eye on the Ruler, drag to the right to about the 2-inch mark and down to the last line of the second paragraph. When you release the mouse button, Word draws a frame the size you indicated, pushing the text to the right to make room, like this:

Creating frames

Now let's insert a graphic in the frame:

1. Move the pointer over the border that surrounds the frame, and when the pointer changes to a four-way arrow, click to select the frame. Word indicates that the frame is selected by surrounding it with black squares, called handles. (Or simply click an insertion point inside the frame.)
2. Choose Picture from the Insert menu. Word displays the dialog box shown on the next page.

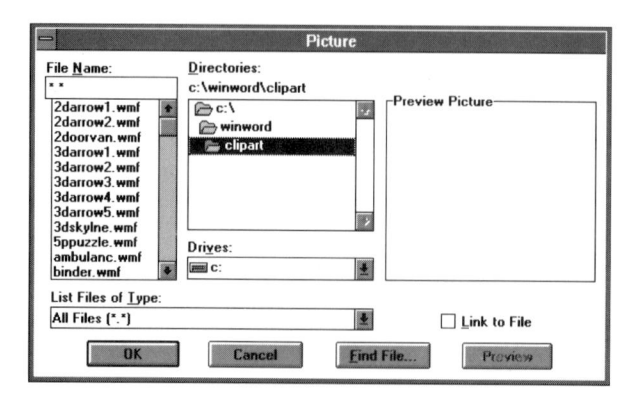

3. If necessary, double-click the directory containing the graphics files (CLIPART, in this case).
4. Scroll to the bottom of the File Name list box, and select WOMAN.WMF. (You can click Preview to have a look at the picture before inserting it.) Click OK. After a few seconds, Word inserts the graphic in the frame, and this is what you see:

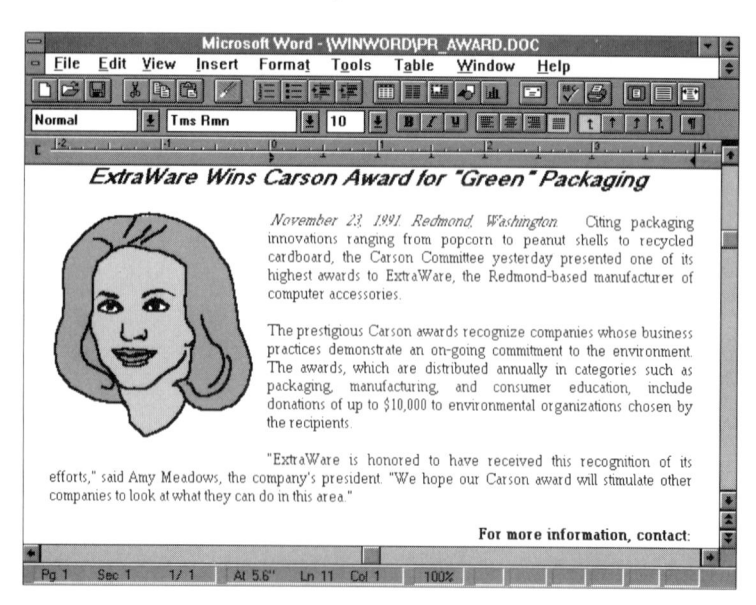

Changing the Graphic's Size

After you import the graphic, you can change its size and shape to suit the needs of your document. For example, you might want to turn the graphic into a small logo, or you might want to enlarge it so that it occupies most of the page. Let's experiment a bit:

1. Select the graphic by clicking it.

2. To decrease the graphic's size, position the insertion point on the handle in the bottom-right corner, and when the pointer changes to a two-way arrow, drag it upward and to the left until the graphic is the size you want it.

Using handles

If you drag the corner handles, you change the size of the graphic without changing the ratio of its width and height. If you drag the handles in the middle of the sides of the graphic frame, you change this ratio. You can change the ratio more precisely by choosing a command. Try this:

1. With the graphic selected, choose Picture from the Format menu. Word displays this dialog box:

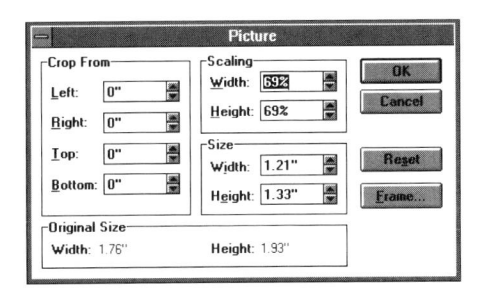

2. In the Scaling section, set the Width option to 50% and the Height option to 100%, and click OK. The result is shown on the next page.

Changing width and height ratios

Turning off graphics display

Inserting graphics in a document slows down the rate at which you can scroll through the text. To increase the scrolling speed: **1.** Choose Options from the Tools menu. **2.** Click the View icon. **3.** Select Picture Placeholders to temporarily substitute placeholders for the actual graphics. **4.** Click OK. Reverse this procedure to turn on graphics display. ♦

Installing graphics filters

The variety of graphics formats that Word can import is determined by the graphics filters installed. If these filters were not installed with Word, you can run the Word Setup program to install them. Select the Custom Installation option, and clear all the check boxes except for Text Conversions/ Graphics Filters. ♦

Manual installation

You can install graphics filters manually by copying them from the installation disk and decompressing them. Read the file called GRAPHICS.DOC stored in your WINWORD directory for information on corresponding changes that you must make to your WIN.INI file if you install manually. ♦

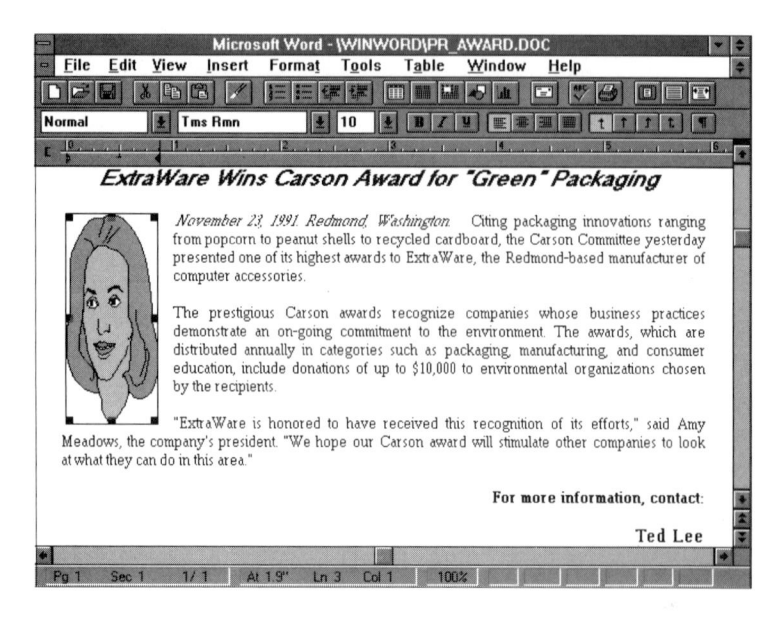

If you want to use only part of the graphic, you can change the size of the frame that contains the graphic without changing the size of the graphic itself. This adjustment has the effect of "cropping" away the parts of the graphic that you don't want to be visible. Follow these steps:

Cropping graphics

1. With the graphic selected, point to the handle in the middle of the bottom of the graphic frame, hold down the Shift key, and drag upward. The message *Cropping* appears in the status bar. When you release the mouse button, this is what you see:

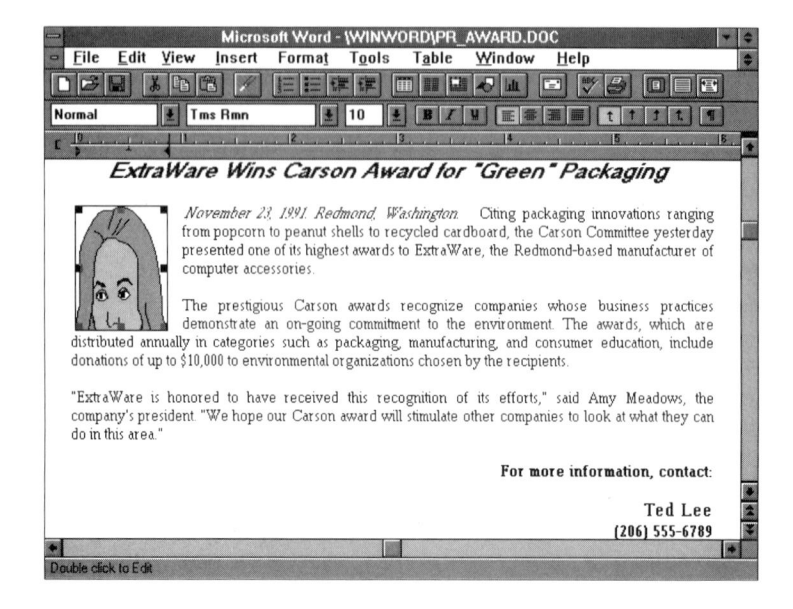

2. Choose Picture from the Format menu. Notice in the Crop From section of the Picture dialog box that Word has changed the Bottom setting to reflect the new position of the bottom of the frame.
3. Change the Bottom setting to 0. In the Scaling section, change both the Width and Height settings to 100%, and then click OK. Word returns the graphic to its original uncropped size and proportions.
4. If your printer can handle graphics, print the press release. Then save the document without changing its name by clicking the Save button on the Toolbar.

Creating Tables

Tables provide visual summaries of information and enable us to quickly grasp relationships that might be lost in narrative explanations. Creating tables in Word for Windows is a simple process. You specify the number of columns and rows and then leave it to Word to figure out the initial settings.

To demonstrate how easy the process is, let's create a simple four-column by six-row table. Follow these steps:

1. Click the Normal View button, and then click the New button on the Toolbar to start a new document.
2. Click the Tables button, which then expands to display this grid:

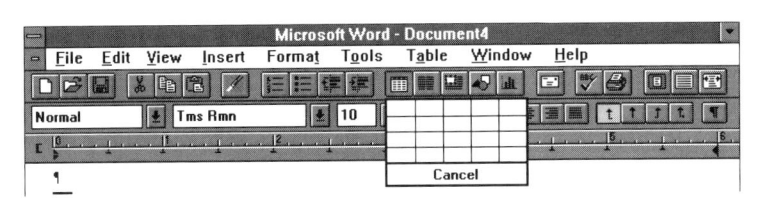

Setting up tables

3. Drag the pointer across four columns and down six rows. (The grid expands as you drag beyond its bottom edge.) Word shows the size of the selection below the grid. When you release the mouse button, the table shown on the next page appears in the document.

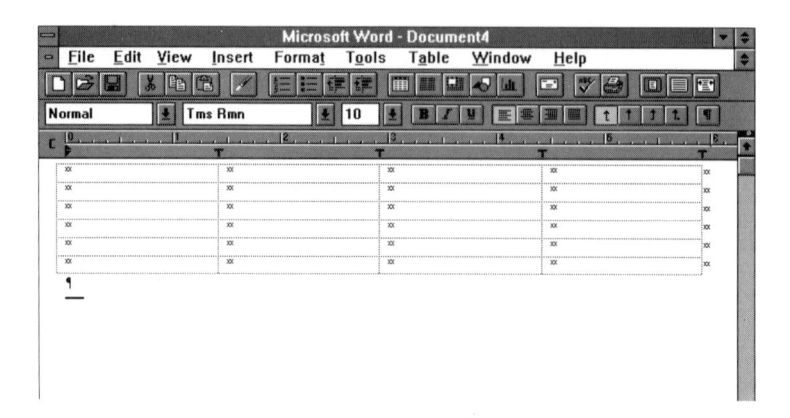

As you can see, Word has created a table with four equal columns that together span the width of your document's text column. The insertion point is in the first cell (the intersection of the first column of the first row). The gridlines around the cells are visual guides only; they will not print.

Entering table text

1. To make an entry in this cell, all you have to do is type. For example, to enter the column headings, type *Contributor* in the first cell, and press Tab. The insertion point moves to the cell to the right. Type *Sulfur Dioxide*, and press Tab to move to the next cell. Type *Carbon Monoxide*, and press Tab. Finally, type *Nitrogen Oxides*, and press Tab. Here's the result so far:

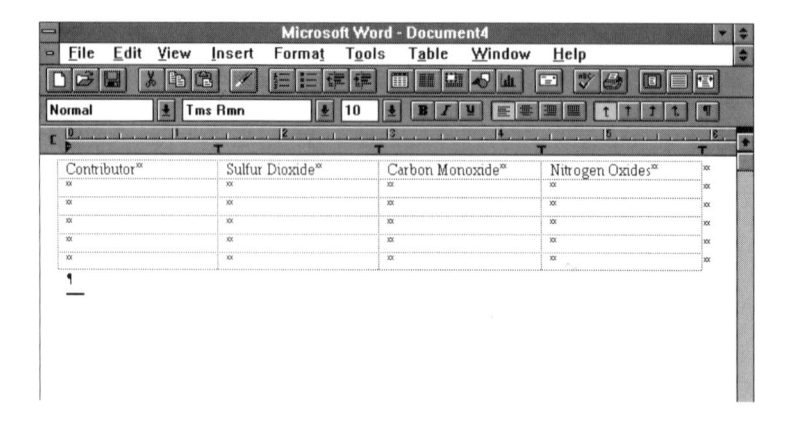

Pressing Tab at the end of the first row moved the insertion point to the first cell in the second row.

2. Finish the table by typing the entries shown on the facing page, pressing Tab to move from cell to cell. (Pressing Shift-Tab moves the insertion point to the previous cell, and you can also use the Arrow keys to move around.)

Navigating in tables

Transportation	0.9	41.2	8.1
Industrial Emissions	3.4	4.7	0.6
Fuel Combustion	16.4	7.6	10.8
Solid-Waste Burning	--	1.7	0.1
Miscellaneous	--	6.0	0.2

Looking over the table, you can see one or two changes that would make it more effective. We discuss ways to edit tables next.

Rearranging the Table

You can rearrange the rows and columns in a table in much the same way that you rearrange text. Follow these steps to move the Carbon Monoxide column to the left of the Sulfur Dioxide column:

1. Move the pointer above the third column and, when the pointer changes to a downward-pointing arrow, click the mouse button to select the column.
2. Click the Cut button on the Toolbar. The column disappears.
3. Click an insertion point in the first row of the second column, and then click the Paste button. Word inserts the Carbon Monoxide column to the left of the Sulfur Dioxide column, as shown here:

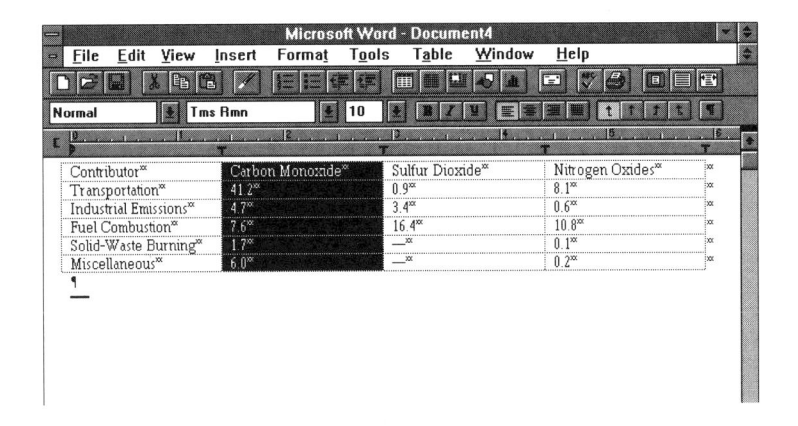

Changing Column Width

You can adjust column widths to suit your needs, by using menu options or moving the margin and column markers on the Ruler. Follow the steps on the next page to change the widths of some of the columns in the example table.

Changing column widths →

1. With the insertion point located anywhere in the table, drag the left-indent marker (▸) to the 1-inch mark on the ruler. Word moves the table over by 1 inch.
2. Next drag the first column marker (which looks like a bold T) to the 2.5-inch mark on the Ruler. Word adjusts the width of the first column to reflect the change.
3. Drag the second column marker to the 3.25-inch mark, the third column marker to the 4-inch mark, and the fourth column marker to the 4.75-inch mark. This is the result:

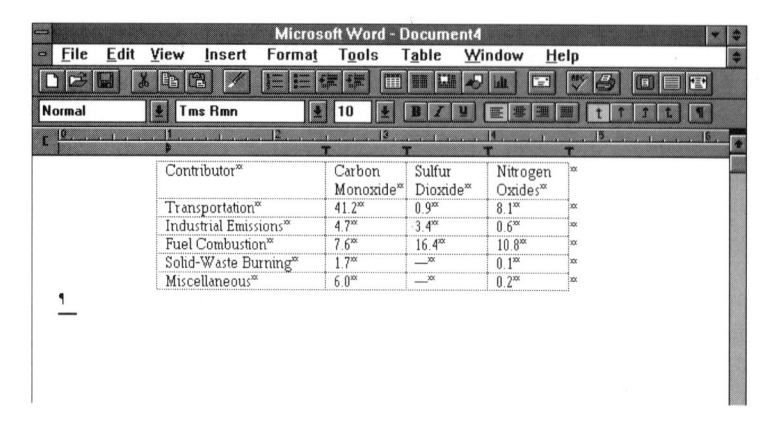

As you can see, the headings in the second, third, and fourth columns have wrapped to two lines. This is because Word's default row-height setting is Auto, meaning that Word will wrap entries that are too long to fit in their cells to as many lines as necessary to display the entries in their

---

New rows shortcut

You can quickly insert blank rows in a table by selecting the same number of rows you want to insert and then clicking the Table button on the Toolbar. Word inserts the new rows above the selection. You can add new rows to the end of a table by placing the insertion point before the end-of-cell marker in the last cell and pressing Tab. ♦

Deleting rows and columns

To delete one or more rows or columns: **1.** Select the rows or columns. **2.** Choose Delete Rows or Delete Columns from the Table menu. To delete the entire table, select it before choosing the command. If you don't select rows or columns first, Word displays a dialog box in which you can specify what you want to delete. ♦

Clearing contents

To clear the contents of a table: **1.** Choose Select Table from the Table menu to select the entire table. **2.** Press the Del key. ♦

entirety. If you want all entries to appear on only one line, select the table, and choose Row Height from the Table menu. Then select Exactly from the Height Of Row list, and specify 1 in the At box.

Setting row height

Inserting Rows

Suppose you want to add a row above the table to contain a title. The first step is to insert a new row:

1. Move the pointer into the selection bar adjacent to the first row of the table, and click to select the entire row.
2. Choose the Insert Rows command from the Table menu. Word automatically inserts the number of rows you have selected—in this case, one—above the selection and highlights the new row.

Joining Cells

Next, you need to join the cells of the new row to create one large cell to accommodate the table's title. Joining cells is a simple procedure, as you'll see if you follow these steps:

1. With the first row of the table selected, choose Merge Cells from the Table menu. Word merges the cells into one large cell that spans the table.
2. Now finish the task by entering the title. This is easier to do if you can see paragraph marks in the table. If you can't see them, click the ¶ button on the Ribbon to turn on nonprinting characters. Then click an insertion

---

Splitting a table	Turning off gridlines	Caution: Hidden text
To break a table into two sections: **1.** Select the row above which you want to insert the break. **2.** Choose Split Table from the Table menu. Word inserts a blank paragraph between the two new tables. ♦	The gridlines that form cell boundaries don't print, but they can help you visualize the structure of your table. To get an idea of how the table will look when printed, choose Gridlines from the Table menu to turn off the gridlines. ♦	Word won't print hidden text, so you must use caution when adjusting the width of columns if the Height Of Row option is set to Exactly and 1. If you make a column so narrow that you truncate entries, you may not notice the problem until you print and proofread the table. ♦

point in front of the first paragraph mark, and type *AIR-POLLUTANT SOURCES*.

3. Click an insertion point in front of the second paragraph mark, and type *In Millions of Metric Tons*.
4. Get rid of the last two lines in the cell by pressing the Del button twice. This is the result:

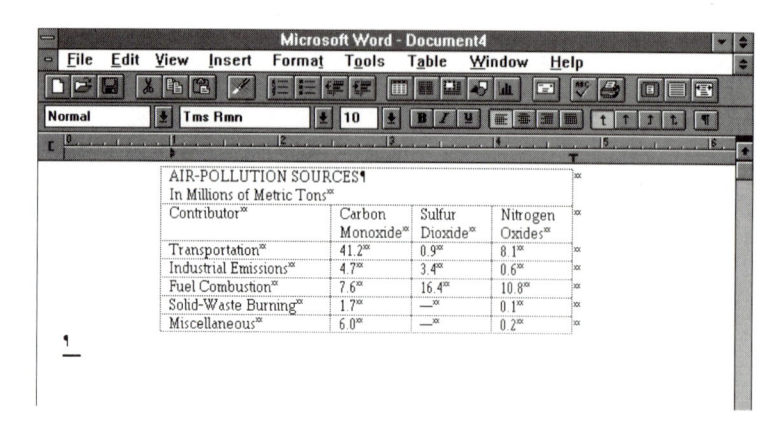

Formatting Tables

Having made all the necessary structural changes to the table, let's add a few finishing touches. First, we'll format the title and headings:

Centering table text

1. Select the first two rows of the table, and click the Center button.

Making titles and headings bold

2. To make the title and headings in the *Contributor* column bold, point to the gridline above the title, click to select the first column, and then click the Bold button. (Although the cell containing the title spans all four columns, Word considers it to be the first cell in the first column.)

Well that was simple. Now let's see how to align the numbers in the second, third, and fourth columns on the decimal point. This involves setting decimal tabs in each of these columns. Follow the steps below:

Turning on table scale

1. Click an insertion point anywhere in the table, and switch the Ruler to table scale by clicking the icon at the left end of the Ruler until a bold T is displayed.
2. To align the numbers in the *Carbon Monoxide* column on the decimal point, drag through the five cells containing numbers in that column to select them. Word

Chapter 4 Graphic Impact: Graphics, Tables, Charts, and Spreadsheets   93

resets the scale on the Ruler so that 0 is above the start of this column.

3. Click the Decimal Tab button on the ribbon, and click the Ruler at around the 3/8-inch mark.

Decimal alignment

4. Repeat the previous step to decimal-align the numbers in the *Sulfur Dioxide* and *Nitrogen Oxides* columns. The table now looks like this:

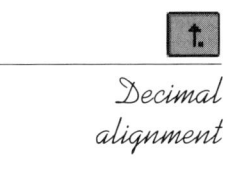

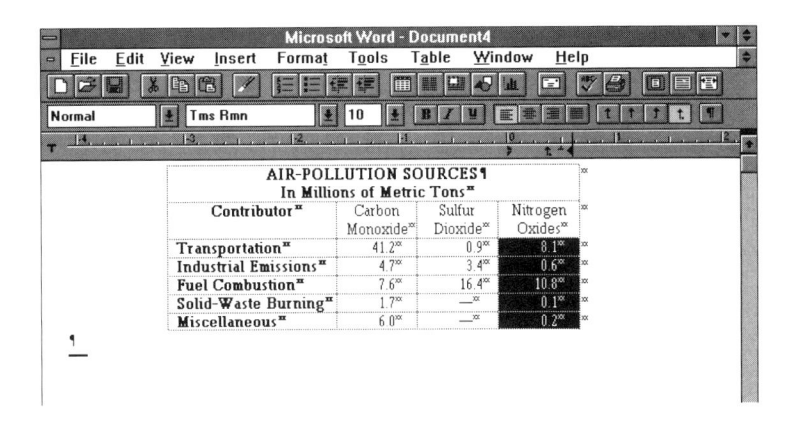

Before we wrap up this section, let's add gridlines to the cells and put a border around the whole table:

1. With the insertion point anywhere in the table, choose Select Table from the Table menu. Then choose Border from the Format menu. Word displays this dialog box:

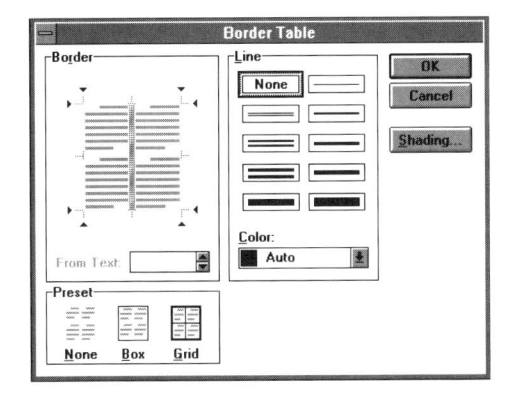

2. In the Preset section, click Grid. Then select the second double line in the Line section, and click OK.

Adding gridlines

3. Next, select the title row, and again choose Border. In the Preset section, click Box. Check that the second double line in the Line section is selected, and click OK. The result is shown on the next page.

Adding a border

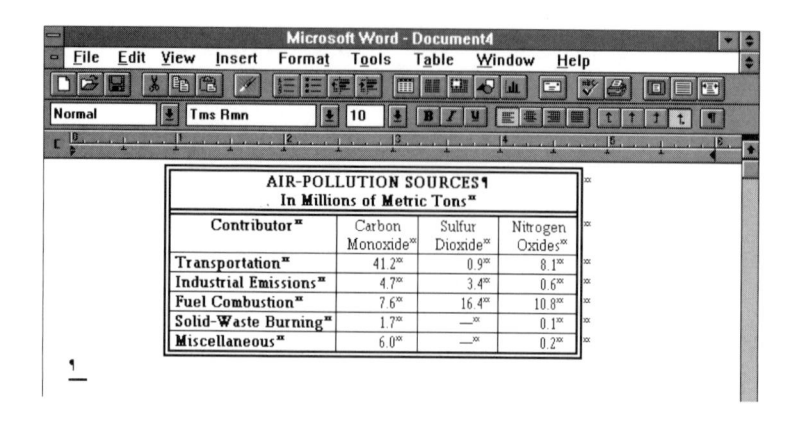

	AIR-POLLUTION SOURCES		
	In Millions of Metric Tons		
Contributor	Carbon Monoxide	Sulfur Dioxide	Nitrogen Oxides
Transportation	41.2	0.9	8.1
Industrial Emissions	4.7	3.4	0.6
Fuel Combustion	7.6	16.4	10.8
Solid-Waste Burning	1.7	—	0.1
Miscellaneous	6.0	—	0.2

4. To see how the table looks on the page, display it in Print Preview.
5. Now save the document by clicking the Save button and assigning the name *tables.doc* to the file.

Creating Charts

Word for Windows allows you to cut or copy charts and graphs from other applications and then paste them into a Word document. But Word also provides a charting program with which you can create charts based on information in your Word document. Let's briefly explore this capability using the table you just completed. Follow these steps:

Selecting data to chart

1. Using the mouse in the selection bar, select rows two through seven of the table (in other words, select everything but the title). Then click the Chart button on the

---

Putting text beside the table

To put text adjacent to a table: **1.** Choose Page Layout from the View menu to switch to Page Layout view. **2.** Insert a frame adjacent to the table. **3.** Click an insertion point in the frame, and type and format your text as usual. Word will wrap the text within the frame. ♦

Turning a table into tabular text

To convert a table to tabular text: **1.** Choose Select Table from the Table menu to select the entire table. **2.** Then choose the Convert Table To Text command from the Table menu. Word removes the table grid and separates text that was in columns with tabs. ♦

Turning existing text into a table

To turn a block of regular text separated by tabs into a table: **1.** Select all the tab-delimited text. **2.** Click the Tables button on the Toolbar. (You can also choose Convert Text To Table from the Table menu.) ♦

Chapter 4 Graphic Impact: Graphics, Tables, Charts, and Spreadsheets

Toolbar. After a few seconds, Word loads the charting program, and your screen looks like this:

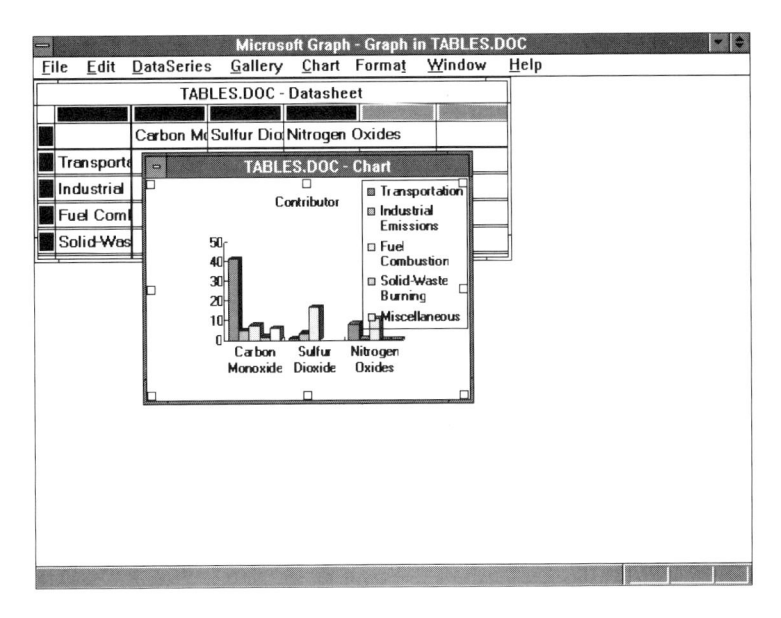

Not a bad beginning, but the chart obviously needs some adjustments.

2. To instruct the charting program to plot the data by the pollutants in the table's columns instead of by the contributing sources in the table's rows, choose Series In Columns from the DataSeries menu.
3. To plot the data as a bar chart (horizontally) instead of as a column chart (vertically), choose Bar from the Gallery menu. Word displays this assortment of bar-chart formats:

Creating a bar chart

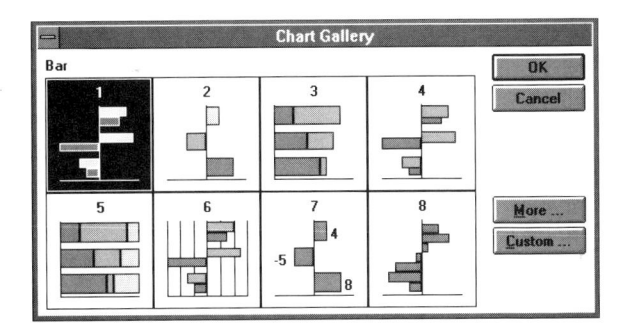

4. Click OK to plot the data in the default (highlighted) format.
5. So that all the labels on the vertical axis can be displayed, let's make the chart window a little bigger. Move the pointer over the bottom-right corner of the chart window until it changes to a two-way arrow. Then drag the window's right border to the right. Experiment with its position until it looks like this:

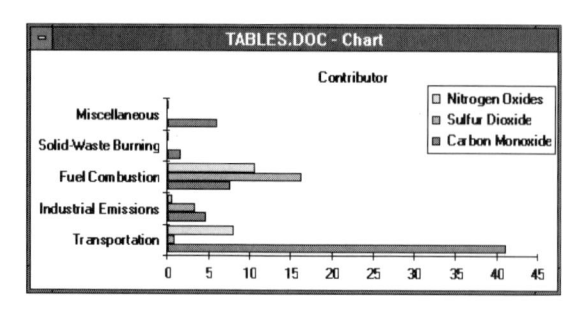

Expanding the chart window

6. Click the legend in the top-right corner to select it, position the pointer anywhere over the legend, and drag downward and inward.
7. Now let's change the chart title. Drag through the word *Contributor*, and press Backspace to delete the word. Then type *AIR-POLLUTANT SOURCE*, press Enter, and type *In Millions of Metric Tons*. Click anywhere else on the chart so that the title text can adjust itself within its frame.

Editing chart titles

With these adjustments completed, you can close the charting program and paste the chart into TABLES.DOC.

1. From the charting program's File menu, choose Exit And Return To TABLES.DOC.
2. When the program asks whether you want to update your document, click Yes. That's all there is to it. When you return to your document window, the chart has been inserted at the insertion point, below the table.
3. Move the pointer over the chart, and click to select it. Then choose Border from the Format menu, select Box in the Preset section and the second double line in the Line section, and click OK.
4. Click the ¶ button to turn off nonprinting symbols so that you can truly appreciate the result:

Pasting the chart in the document

Adding borders to charts

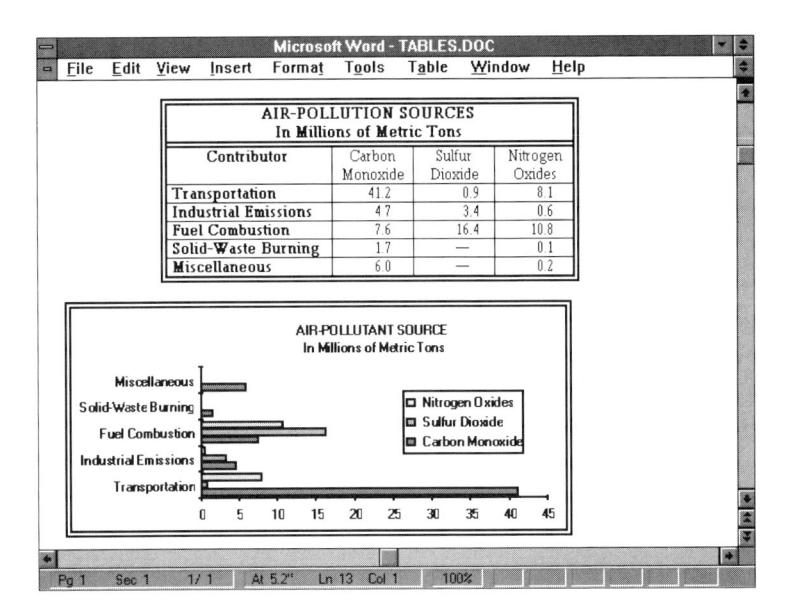

Chapter 4 Graphic Impact: Graphics, Tables, Charts, and Spreadsheets

AIR-POLLUTION SOURCES In Millions of Metric Tons				
Contributor	Carbon Monoxide	Sulfur Dioxide	Nitrogen Oxides
Transportation	41.2	0.9	8.1
Industrial Emissions	4.7	3.4	0.6
Fuel Combustion	7.6	16.4	10.8
Solid-Waste Burning	1.7	—	0.1
Miscellaneous	6.0	—	0.2

5. If you want, you can choose Paragraph from the Format menu and set a left indent to nudge the chart into esthetic alignment with the table.

To edit a chart, simply double-click it to return to the charting program. You can then reformat the chart and change its type. (You can also import and edit an existing Excel chart using the charting program.)

Although Word's built-in charting program doesn't offer all the capabilities of dedicated programs, you will often find that it is all you need to quickly generate visual representations of your data. You might want to spend a little more time experimenting with this program, using your own data or the simple table we have created in this chapter.

Importing Spreadsheets

Although Word allows you to create impressive tables and do some mathematics with ease, it doesn't calculate complex formulas and functions the way a spreadsheet program does. And although a spreadsheet program is great for performing calculations, it lacks the word-processing capabilities you need to put together dynamic reports. Suppose you have gone to a lot of trouble to create a spreadsheet and you want to include the spreadsheet's data in a report. It would be frustrating to have to rekey all that information into a Word table for presentation. Fortunately, you don't have to. With Word for Windows, you can combine the best of both worlds—the numeric know-how of a spreadsheet program with the word-processing proficiency of Word.

To demonstrate, we'll import this spreadsheet, which was created with Microsoft Excel for Windows:

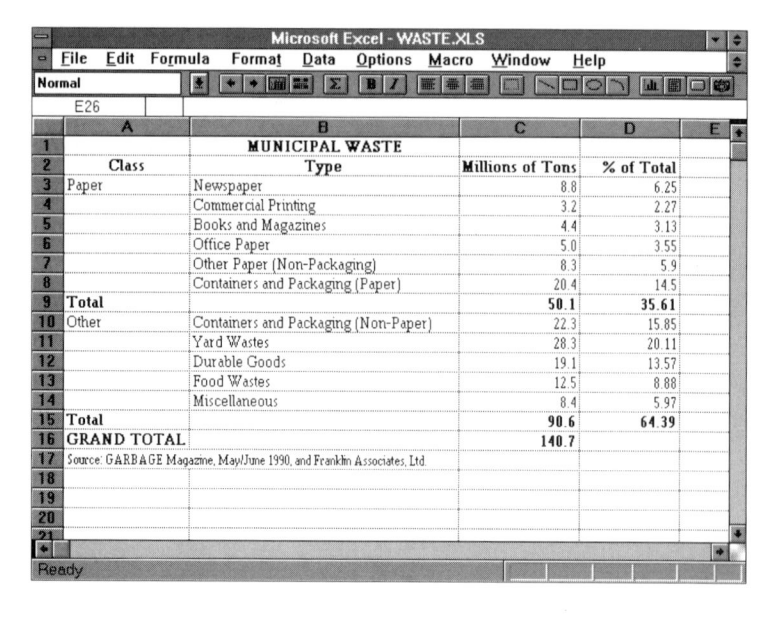

You can follow these steps with your own spreadsheet file:

1. Press Ctrl-End to move to the end of the document now on your screen. Press Enter several times to insert blank lines and give yourself some room to move.
2. Choose File from the Insert menu. Word displays the Insert File dialog box shown earlier on page 60.

Supported spreadsheet formats

Currently, files from the spreadsheet programs listed below can be imported into Word for Windows documents:

Microsoft Excel for Windows
Lotus 1-2-3
dBASE
Microsoft Works
Microsoft Multiplan ♦

Linking spreadsheets

To create a dynamic link between a spreadsheet file and a Word document: **1.** Choose File from the Insert menu. **2.** Select the spreadsheet you want to import. **3.** Click the Link To File option, and then click OK.

You can also establish a link by copying the data from the spreadsheet application and choosing Paste Special from Word's Edit menu.

If the information in the linked spreadsheet changes, you can update the same information in the Word document by choosing the Links command from the Edit menu. ♦

3. From the Files Of Type drop-down list box, select All Files (*.*). Then select the directory in which the spreadsheet you want to import is stored, and double-click the spreadsheet file you want to import. Word displays this dialog box:

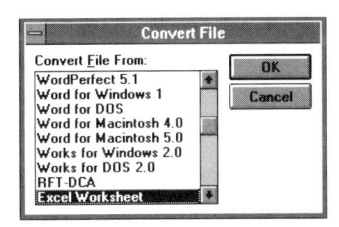

4. As you can see, Word has detected that WASTE.XLS is an Excel Worksheet. Click OK. Word displays another dialog box asking whether you want to import the entire spreadsheet or only a range. Either accept the default Entire Spreadsheet option, or type the range you want to import. Then click OK to start the conversion process. While Word converts the file, the status bar displays the message *Word is converting, X% complete. Press Esc to Cancel*. When Word finishes, the spreadsheet file is inserted as a table at the insertion point.

Importing a range

You can edit the spreadsheet table using the techniques described earlier. The printout of TABLE.DOC at the beginning of the chapter shows the demonstration spreadsheet after we made a few cosmetic adjustments.

By itself, Word for Windows can create some pretty fancy documents. Add a few graphics and a spreadsheet, and you've got documents with real distinction! Word's ability to import graphics and spreadsheets allows you to tap into valuable outside resources. So be adventurous, and let Word help you generate a report that will make your colleagues sit up and take notice.

5

Reusable Documents: Creating a Letterhead

Designing the Letterhead   102
   Formatting the Letterhead   104
Creating Templates   105
   Saving a Document as a Template   106
   Using Templates   107
Adding Headers and Footers   108
   Creating a Simple Header   109
   Creating a Simple Footer   110
   Formatting Footers   112
   Viewing Headers and Footers   113
   Adjusting the Header and Footer Positions   114

Selecting a template
Page 107

Large fonts
Page 104

Side-by-side paragraphs
Page 103

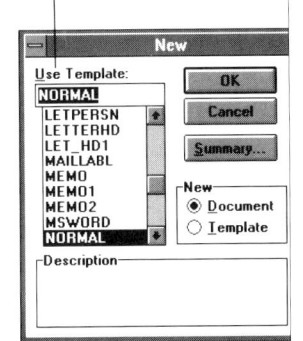

DOT extensions
Page 106

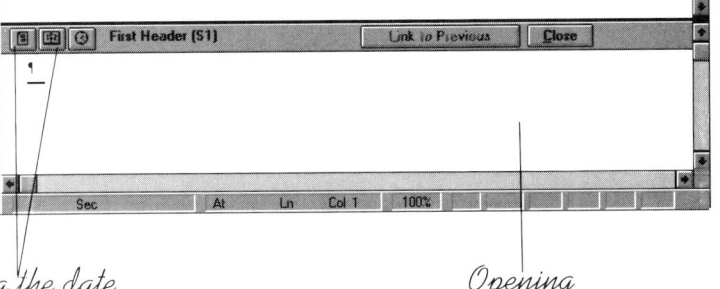

Adding the date and page numbers
Page 111

Opening a footer window
Page 110

Redmond BEAT

14000 Willows Way, Suite 100, Redmond, WA 98052
206-555-6789

ExtraWare Wins Carson Award for "Green" Packaging

Citing packaging innovations ranging from popcorn to peanut shells to recycled cardboard, the Carson Committee[1] yesterday presented one of its highest awards to ExtraWare, the Redmond-based manufacturer of computer accessories.

The prestigious Carson awards recognize companies whose business practices demonstrate an on-going commitment to the environment. The awards, which are distributed annually in categories such as packaging, manufacturing, and consumer education, include donations of up to $10,000 to environmental organizations chosen by the recipients.

"ExtraWare is honored to have received this recognition of its efforts," said Amy Meadows, the company's president. "We hope our Carson award will stimulate other companies to look at what they can do in this area."

REDMOND BUSINESS ENVIRONMENTAL ACTION TEAM

What is Redmond BEAT?
Redmond BEAT (Business Environmental Action Team) is a local chapter of USA BEAT, a network of companies who are actively working to ensure that their business operations are based on sound environmental practices.

How does it work?
Member companies agree to participate in two outgoing efforts:
1. They pledge to scrutinize their operations and, whenever possible, implement procedures that will minimize any adverse effects on the environment.
2. They agree to field-test new "environmentally kind" products and services to evaluate their potential impact on both company costs and the environment.

When was it started?
USA BEAT, which currently has 210 local chapters, was founded in 1989.

Why was it started?
The chartering of Redmond BEAT was spearheaded by William Henry, President of Creative Glassworks. Struck by the incongruity between his family's efforts to recycle household waste and the fact that his company was sending several dumpsters of garbage to the landfill every month, Henry began looking for other ways to dispose of the packaging in which his company received raw materials. His questions caused one of his suppliers, Jordon Manufacturing, to explore alternative packaging methods. The result was less garbage in the Creative GlassWorks dumpsters at no additional cost and negligible other effects for either company. In the meantime, Henry learned about USA BEAT, and a few months of persuasive campaigning later, Redmond BEAT became the newest chapter of a rapidly growing national association.

Who can join?
Membership in Redmond BEAT is open to all companies licensed to do business in the city of Redmond.

Why should my company join?
Current members cite two main reasons for joining. Many companies are managed by people who are attracted to this area by its natural beauty and who want to be part of the effort to preserve it. Other companies stress the potential advantages in today's competitive markets of being perceived as a "green" company by consumers who are increasingly environmentally aware.

How can I find out more?
Come to a meeting. Redmond BEAT meets at 8:00 AM on the last Tuesday of every month in the Community Center. For more information, contact Ted Lee at 555-6789.

---

[1] Author of *The Silent Spring*, an apocryphal vision of the results of people's thoughtless manipulation of the environment for their own short-term needs, Rachel Carson was a revered pioneer environmentalist.

As you use Word for Windows in your daily work, you will probably find yourself creating the same kinds of documents over and over again. Memos, letters, newsletters—every day, every week, every month. What you create and how often will depend on your job. But regardless, you won't want to start from scratch every time. You'll want to set up the document format once so that you can reuse it whenever you need to create that particular kind of document.

Word templates

That's where Word templates come in. You can set up a document, save it as a template, and then open a new document based on that template every time you need to create that type of document. The new document faithfully reflects the margins and formatting of the original and even makes available any styles, dictionaries, and glossaries you have assigned to the template. (We discussed styles on page 69, dictionaries on page 51, and glossaries on page 37.) All you have to do is type the text and make any special adjustments necessary for this particular document. Word takes care of everything else for you.

Obviously, before all this magic can happen, you have to create the template, and that's what this chapter is all about. We'll first use some of the techniques covered in Chapters 3 and 4 to create a letterhead. Then we'll load a copy of the template and merge in the flyer from Chapter 3 so that you can see how easy it would be to use the template to create a flyer each month. Finally, we'll create a template that includes headers and footers.

Designing the Letterhead

Most companies require their employees to use preprinted letterhead stationery. The disadvantage of preprinted letterhead is that you have to switch the paper in your printer to use it. If you have a laser printer, you can print your documents with a computer-generated letterhead in place, without having to worry about what kind of paper is loaded in the printer.

You can use Word to create an impressive and versatile letterhead that sports any font your printer can print. You can

Chapter 5   Reusable Documents: Creating a Letterhead

include a logo imported from a drawing or painting program or created in the graphics program that comes with Word for Windows version 2. We're going to stick to something pretty basic here. If you have a laser printer and you follow our instructions, your letterhead will look like this:

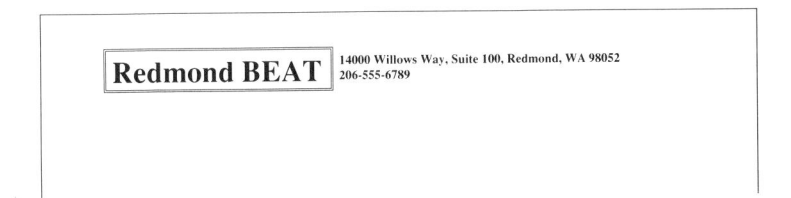

Feel free to experiment if you want your correspondence to convey a more flamboyant image. Let's get started:

1. Open a new document.
2. To create the letterhead's side-by-side paragraphs, click the Table button on the Toolbar, and create a one-row-by-two-column table.

    Side-by-side paragraphs

3. Type *Redmond BEAT* in the first cell, and press Tab to move to the second cell.
4. Type *14000 Willows Way, Suite 100, Redmond, WA 98052* in the second cell, and press Enter.
5. Type *206-555-6789* on the next line of the second cell. Your table should now look like this:

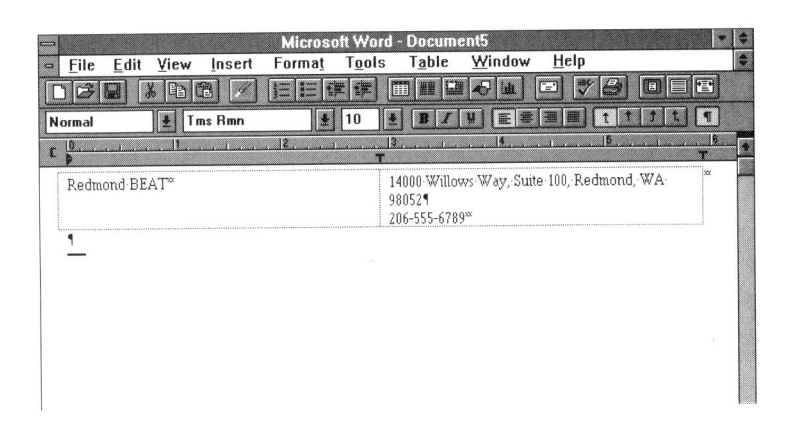

Don't worry if your text wraps within cells; we'll make adjustments in a moment.

Formatting the Letterhead

With the text of the letterhead in place, let's see what we can do to make it look more impressive. Follow these steps:

1. If you can't see the table gridlines, choose Gridlines from the Table menu. These nonprinting lines make it easier to adjust the size and formatting of the table.
2. Choose Page Setup from the Format menu, change the top margin to *.5*, and change both the left and right margins to *1*. Then click OK.
3. Move the insertion point over the right edge of the right cell (the insertion point changes to a double bar with opposing arrows), and drag the right border of the cell until it aligns with the 6.5-inch mark on the Ruler. (You may have to use the horizontal scroll bar to bring this part of the Ruler into view.) All the text of the address should now be on one line.
4. Move the insertion point over the top gridline of the left cell (the insertion point changes to a downward-pointing arrow), and click to select the cell containing the words *Redmond BEAT*. Then use the Ribbon to change the character format to 24-point Tms Rmn Bold. (If your printer doesn't support large fonts, see the tip about WordArt below.)

Large fonts →

5. With the left cell still selected, choose Paragraph from the Format menu, type *3 pt* in the Before text box, and click OK.

WordArt

Stashed away in the dialog box produced when you choose Objects from the Insert menu is a great program called WordArt. This program helps you produce striking printed effects with almost any printer. You can enter a word or phrase, select from 19 fonts in sizes ranging from 6 to 128 points, and then have the program arrange your words in interesting patterns. When you quit WordArt, Word inserts your design as an object in your document. You can then resize it and move it just like any other object. To edit an existing WordArt object, simply double-click it to load both the WordArt program and the object.

You can use a WordArt object or combine several objects to prduce a logo in a header or to produce text that is larger than the sizes supported by your printer. ♦

Online Press

6. Again, with the cell selected, choose Border from the Format menu. Click Box in the Preset section, select the first double line in the Line section, and click OK.
7. Choose Column Width from the Table menu, set the width to 2.5 inches, and then click OK.
8. Select the address and phone number in the right cell, and click the Bold button.
9. Select just the address (which should be on one line), choose Paragraph from the Format menu, type *3 pt* in the Before text box, and click OK. The letterhead now looks like this:

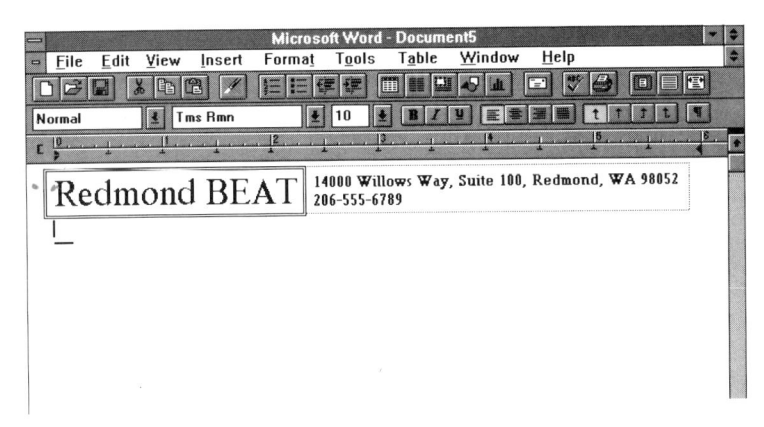

10. Save your work by clicking the Save button on the Toolbar, assigning the name *letterhd.doc*, and clicking OK. Fill in the Summary Info dialog box with identifying information, and again click OK.

Creating Templates

A Word for Windows template is a pattern that can contain information, formatting, macros, and styles that are used in a particular type of document. All Word for Windows documents are based on a template: If you don't specify otherwise, they are based on the Normal template. Word comes with several other templates (see Chapter 6), which you can use as is or modify; or you can create your own templates. Once you have created a template, you can open a new document based on that template, giving you a jump-start on formatting the new document. You can then save the document without affecting the template on which it is based.

Saving a Document as a Template

The letterhead is now pretty much complete, so let's save it again, this time as a reuseable template. Here's how:

1. Choose Save As from the File menu.
2. Pull down the Save File As Type list box, and select Document Template (*.dot). The Save As dialog box changes to look like this:

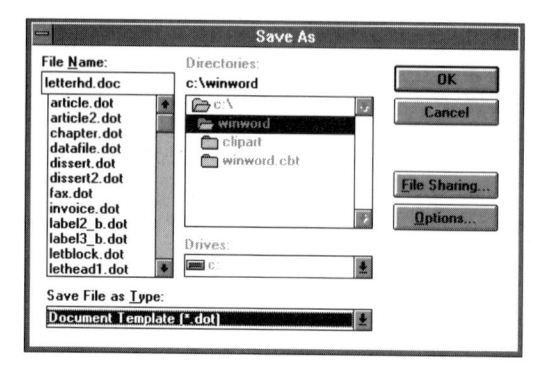

Storing new templates →

Notice that Word forces you to store a new template in your WINWORD directory so that the program can always find it.

3. In the File Name text box, type *let_hd1*, and click OK. Word automatically appends the extension DOT to the filename to indicate that the file is a template and displays a Summary Info dialog box.

DOT extensions →

4. Type *Letterhead without header/footer* in the Title text box, and click OK.

Creating new templates

If you know you want to create a template, use the New command on the File menu as usual. Then, in the New dialog box, select Template instead of Document, and click OK to create a new template. Word opens a blank document window that has the name Template1, rather than Document1. Other than the name, the template is a perfectly normal document, and you can do anything in it that you would do in any other document. However, saving the document creates a new template that can be used as the basis for all documents of that type. ♦

The Normal template

The Normal template, which is stored in NORMAL.DOT in your WINWORD directory, contains all global styles, glossary entries, macros, and key/menu assignments predefined by Word or created by you. If you mess up NORMAL.DOT, you can restore the original file by deleting or renaming it. Word then creates a new file the next time you start the program. ♦

5. Choose Close from the File menu.

That's all there is to it. Next, let's see how you would use the new template.

Using Templates

To create a new document, you probably click the New button on the Toolbar. Although you might not realize it, new documents created that way are based on Word's Normal template. To create a new document based on a different template, you must use the New command on the File menu.

1. Choose New from the File menu. Word displays this dialog box:

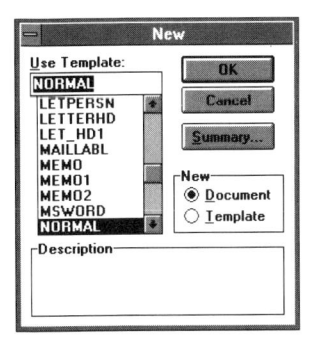

2. Leave Document selected in the New section. Press the up arrow until LET_HD1 is highlighted in the Use Template list box. (Notice that the text in the Description area is the title you typed in the Summary Info dialog box.) Click OK. Word opens a new document that looks just like your template. In essence then, opening a document based on a template is equivalent to opening a copy of a document you use repeatedly.

Selecting a template

You can now write a letter or report or any other document. Instead of typing something, however, let's merge in the flyer you created in Chapter 3.

1. Press Ctrl-End to move to the end of the letterhead document. Then choose File from the Insert menu to display the Insert File dialog box shown on the following page.

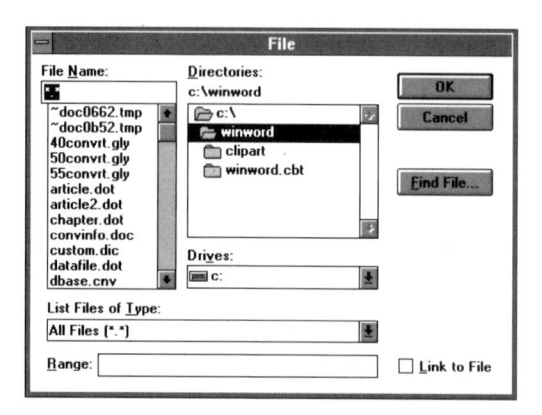

2. Locate FLYER.DOC, and click OK. Word inserts the flyer beneath the letterhead, but because Word has difficulty handling footnotes and section formatting, the three-column section gets bumped to the next page.
3. To take care of this problem, choose Footnote from the Insert menu, click Options, select End Of Document from the Place At list, click OK, and then click Close.
4. Click the Save button on the Toolbar. Although your new document is based on LET_HD1.DOT, it doesn't yet have a name of its own, so type *flyer2.doc* in the File Name text box, and click OK.
5. So that you can admire your handiwork, click the Print button to print the flyer with the letterhead in place. The result is shown at the beginning of the chapter.

You can use this letterhead for correspondence and short communications. But for documents that are longer than one page, you'll probably want to add a header or footer. We show you how to do that next.

Adding Headers and Footers

Headers and footers are printed in the top and bottom margins of the page and usually carry such repeating information as page numbers, dates, and company names. They're invaluable for long documents, such as reports, but can be used to add a professional touch to documents of any length. With Word, you have many header and footer options. You can create:

- Identical headers and footers for every page.
- A different header and footer for the first page.

- Different headers and footers for left (even) and right (odd) pages.
- Different headers and footers for different sections of a document and even for different pages.

For the next letterhead, we'll copy the table you just created to a header that prints on the first page of your document. We will then create a footer that prints on all pages after the first one.

Creating a Simple Header

For this example, we'll start by opening a new document based on the LET_HD1 template. Then we'll cut and paste the letterhead table into the header. Try this:

1. Choose the Close command to remove FLYER2.DOC from the screen, and then open a new document based on the LET_HD1 template.
2. With the insertion point anywhere in the letterhead table, choose Select Table from the Table menu, and then click the Cut button.
3. Choose Header/Footer from the View menu. Word displays this dialog box:

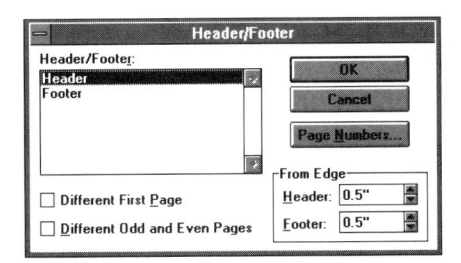

4. Click the Different First Page option. The dialog box changes to look like this:

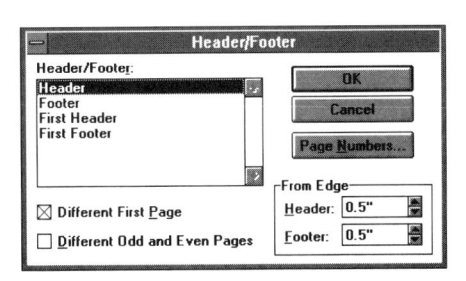

Opening the header window

5. Select First Header, and click OK. Word opens a header window at the bottom of the screen, like this one:

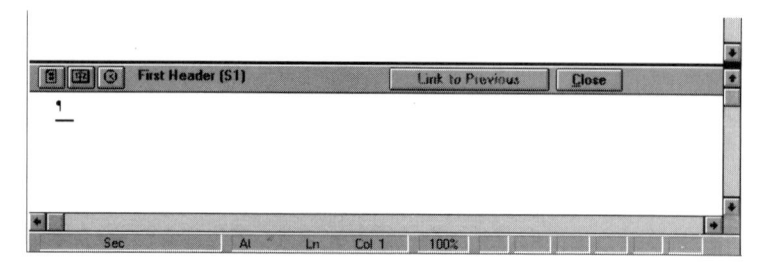

[screenshot: First Header (S1) window with Link to Previous and Close buttons]

6. Choose Paste Cells from the Edit menu to insert the letterhead table in the header window, and then click the Close button to close the window.

That's all there is to it! Your letterhead is now the first-page header for this document.

Creating a Simple Footer

If you produce multipage documents, it's useful to repeat information such as the date and the source of the document on each page. And it's common courtesy to give your readers a quick way to figure out the pages' proper order, in case the dog chases the cat across the dining-room table and scatters pages all over the floor. Follow these steps to create a footer that provides this information:

1. Choose Header/Footer from the View menu. Select Footer, and click OK. Word opens up a footer window just like the header window you saw earlier:

Opening the footer window

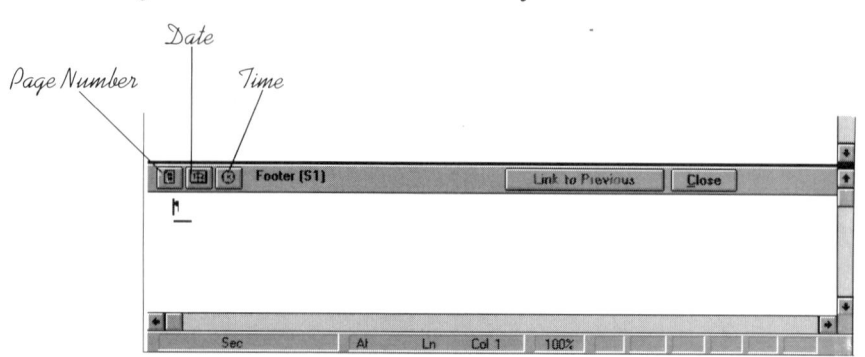

[screenshot: Footer (S1) window with labels pointing to Page Number, Date, and Time buttons, plus Link to Previous and Close buttons]

You can type any text you want in the footer window and you can then format the text in the same way you would format text in the document window. With the

Chapter 5 Reusable Documents: Creating a Letterhead 111

icons in the top-left corner of the header window, you can tell Word to insert the page number, date, and time. When you print the document after inserting these elements, Word inserts the correct page number for each page and fetches the current date and time from your computer's system clock. For the sample footer, we'll put the date on the left, the name of the organization (Redmond BEAT) in the middle, and page numbers on the right.

2. Click the Date button, press Tab, type *Redmond BEAT*, press Tab, and click the Page Number button. The footer window now looks like this:

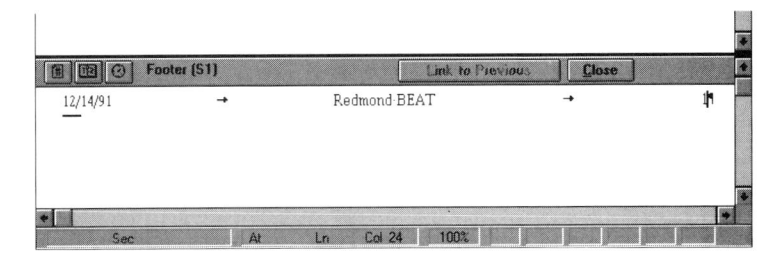

Adding the date and page numbers

On the surface, it seems as though Word has inserted the date at the left end and a page number at the right end of the header. In reality, Word has inserted a date field and a page-number field that tell Word to insert the current date and page number in those locations. To display the fields instead of their results, follow the steps on the next page.

Fields

A field is a code that automatically inserts information or performs a function. Field codes are enclosed in curly braces ({ }).

You can insert a field manually or by choosing Field from the Insert menu and selecting from the displayed list. To insert a field manually: **1.** Position the insertion point where you want to insert the field. **2.** Press Ctrl-F9. Word surrounds the insertion point with braces, and you can then type the field name. For example, to manually insert a date field, press Ctrl-F9, and type *date*.

To display the results of the field rather than the code itself, select the field, and press Shift-F9. If the field result is blank or seems incorrect, press F9 to update the field. You can turn the display of field codes on and off for the entire document by choosing Field Codes from the View menu.

You can format the results of a field code as you would any other text; however, the formatting might be removed when you update the field. To permanently format the text, format the field code.

For a good overview discussion of field codes, highlight Field on the Insert menu, and press F1 to access Help. ♦

Displaying fields

1. With the insertion point in the footer window, choose Field Codes from the View menu. Now the footer window looks like this:

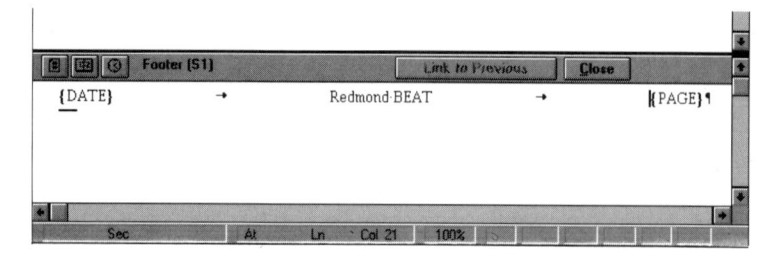

2. Choose Field Codes again to replace the fields with their results. (See the tip on page 111 for more information about fields.)

Formatting Footers

Now let's format the footer so that it stands out on the page. We'll leave the font and size as they are, but we'll make the footer bold and we'll add a line above it.

1. Click once in the footer window's selection bar to select the entire footer, and then click the Bold button.

2. Choose Border from the Format menu. In the Border Paragraphs dialog box, check that None is the Preset option, click the top of the Border diagram to indicate that you want to draw a line only above the paragraph, and select the second single line from the Line options. Here's what the dialog box looks like with these settings:

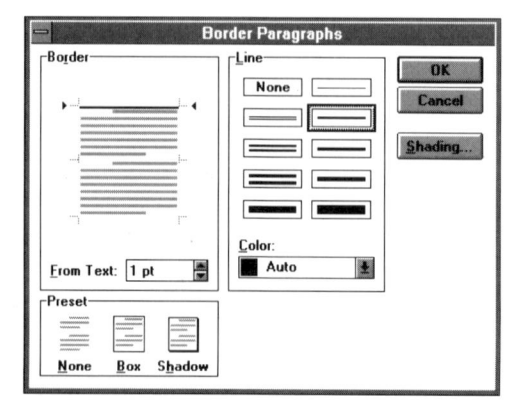

Adding a line

3. Click OK to close the dialog box and add the line.
4. Click the Close button to close the footer window.

Viewing Headers and Footers

Don't be surprised that you can't see the first-page header and the footer on the screen. You haven't lost them. Headers and footers don't show up in Normal view. To see them you need to change to Page Layout view or Print Preview. To see the footer, your document will need to be more than one page long. Let's see how the header and footer would look if you were to print a three-page document right now:

1. To simulate a multipage document, choose Break from the Insert menu, and accept the default Page Break option by clicking OK. Then insert another page break using a different method: Press Ctrl-Enter. Your document now has three blank pages.

    Inserting page breaks

2. Press Ctrl-Home to move to the top of the document, and then choose Print Preview from the File menu. Here is page 1, which has the letterhead as its header:

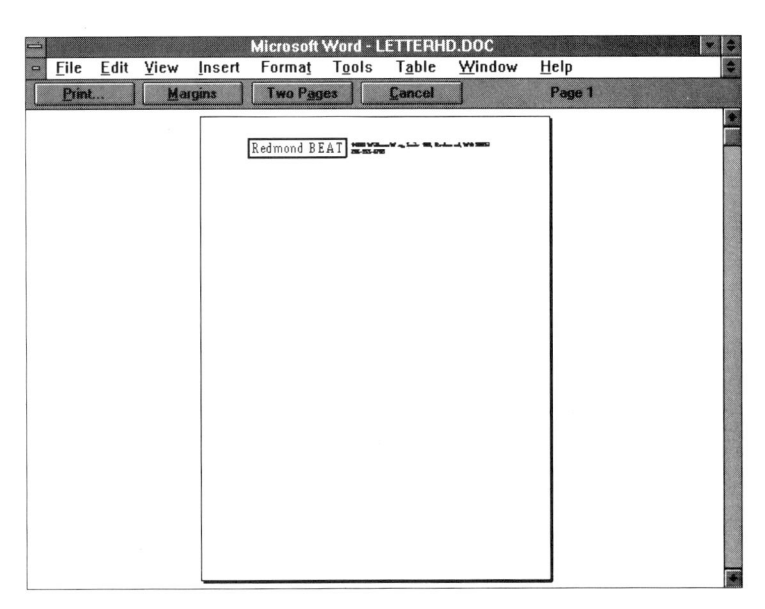

3. Click the Two Pages button, and press PgDn to display the footers of pages 2 and 3, as shown on the next page.

    Viewing a two-page spread

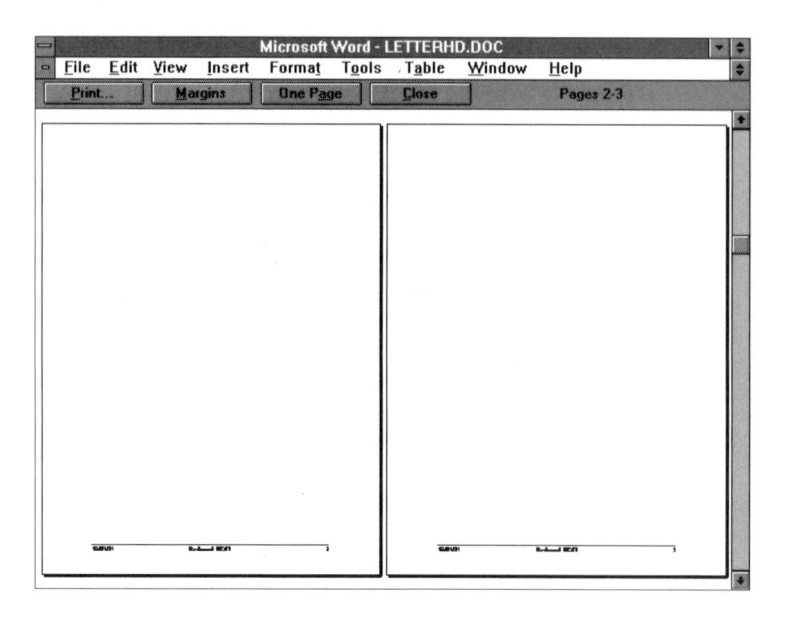

Adjusting the Header and Footer Positions

If you decide that you need to move the header or footer, you can return to the appropriate window and adjust the position with paragraph formats, or you can use the Page Setup command to change the document's top and bottom margins. However, you can also adjust the position of the header or footer visually in Print Preview. Follow these steps to adjust the footer:

Adjusting margins in Print Preview

1. Click the Margins button. Faint grey lines appear, showing the document's margins and the location of the header and footer.

Formatting page numbers

Clicking the Page Numbers button in the Header/Footer dialog box opens the Page Number Format dialog box, where you can select a starting number. You can also select from five numbering schemes. These include Arabic numbers (1, 2, 3), upper-/lowercase letters (A, B, C/ a, b, c), and upper-/lowercase Roman numerals (I, II, III/ i, ii, iii). ♦

Odd and even

You can create different headers and footers for odd and even pages by selecting the Different Odd And Even Pages option in the Header/Footer dialog box. Word then lists Even Header, Even Footer, Odd Header, and Odd Footer in the Header/Footer list. Select one to open the corresponding header or footer window, and then set up the text of the header or footer. For example, you might use this technique to create headers like those at the top of the pages of this book. The headers and footers you create using this option are automatically reflected on all odd and even pages of the document. ♦

Chapter 5 Reusable Documents: Creating a Letterhead

2. Move the pointer into the gray-line box that surrounds the footer. The pointer changes to a cross hair.
3. Drag the footer box down until it is positioned like this:

Repositioning footers in Print Preview

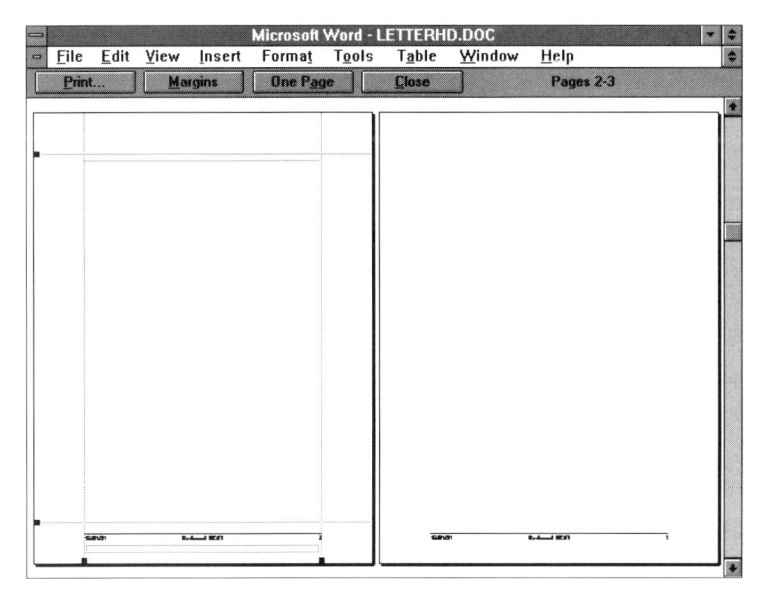

4. Click Margins again to remove the gray lines. Both footers move to the location indicated by the lines.
5. Click the Close button to return to Normal view.
6. Before going any further, remove the two page breaks. (Highlight them using the selection bar, and press Del.)
7. Now save the document as a template, assigning it the name LET_HD2.

The templates you created in this chapter are very simple, but you should now have an idea of what you can do with them. The first template, LET_HD1, allows you to merge in existing files whereas the second, LET_HD2, is an ideal basis for typing new documents. Why have two letterhead templates? If you try to merge an existing file into a document based on LET_HD2, the blank header and footer of the existing file will overwrite the header and footer created by the template, in effect erasing them. Together, the two templates give you greater flexibility.

Before you rush off and create templates for all the types of documents you work with regularly, take a look at Chapter 6, where we explore some of the ready-made templates that come with Word for Windows.

6

More Reusable Documents: Using Word's Templates

Starting the Tour   119
   The Press-Release Template   120
   The Memo Template   122
Modifying Templates   124
   Changing Appearance   125
   Changing Macros   127

Customizing the press release
Page 120

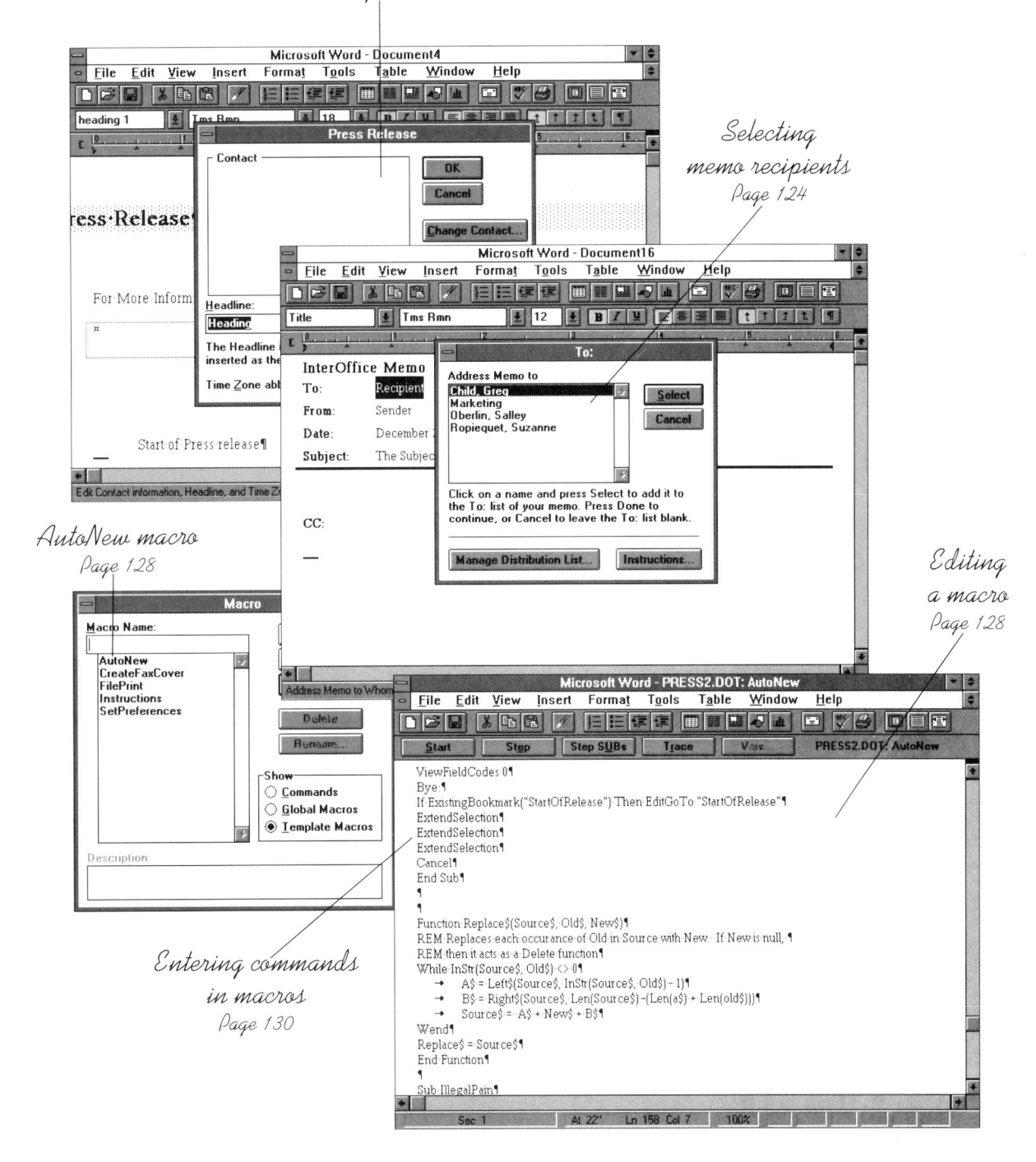

Selecting memo recipients
Page 124

AutoNew macro
Page 128

Editing a macro
Page 128

Entering commands in macros
Page 130

You might think of a template as a kind of electronic hamburger helper: It includes all the basic ingredients; you add the meat and season to taste. In Chapter 5, you created two very simple templates—two letterheads, one of which included a header and footer. From now on, whenever you want to write a letter you can open a new document based on one of these templates to automatically include its standard elements. The same techniques you used to create your letterhead templates can be used to create templates for other types of documents. For example, you could create templates to produce a phone-message form, an invoice, a memo, an order form, and so on.

Templates can include a lot more information than you put in the letterhead. They can put frequently used options at your fingertips and make custom glossaries, dictionaries, and macros available. For example, suppose you sometimes need to set up your display in a certain way when working with a particular type of document. You can create a template that adds that display option as a command on a menu or as a button on the Toolbar so that you don't have to go through layers of dialog boxes to get to it. You can also create new menus. In fact, you can fill almost the entire menu bar with specialized menus holding custom commands. With a little effort, you can create templates that not only produce blank forms but also help you fill them in, by providing dialog boxes that prompt you through the process.

To produce templates like these, you need to know how to use some pretty advanced Word for Windows features, which are beyond the scope of this book. To use custom dialog boxes, for example, you need to know WordBasic, the programming language used to create Word for Windows macros. We aren't going to teach you WordBasic or how to create macros in this book, but we will give you a little taste of what can be done with them.

One of the best ways to learn about the capabilities of any program is to see those capabilities in action. With that thought in mind, this chapter takes you on a tour of a couple of the sample templates supplied with Word for Windows version 2.0. However, you should think of this tour as an appetizer; it's by no means a full meal.

Chapter 6 More Reusable Documents: Using Word's Templates   119

Starting the Tour

When Word for Windows was installed on your computer, one of the options available was to copy sample templates to the directory containing Word. To see a list of these templates and a brief explanation of each one:

Sample templates

1. Choose the New command from the File menu to display this dialog box:

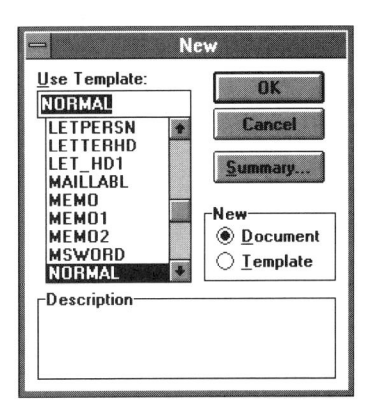

If the only templates listed are Normal and the letterheads you created in Chapter 5, you will have to run the Word for Windows Setup program and install the sample templates in order to follow along with the rest of this chapter. If the sample templates are installed on your hard disk, when you choose the New command you are offered a choice of templates on which to base

---

Installing Word's templates

To run Setup so that you can install Word's template files: **1.** Quit Word. **2.** Insert the Setup disk (Disk 1) in your floppy drive. **3.** Choose Run from the Program Manager File menu, and then type *drive:\setup*, where *drive* is the drive containing the disk. **4.** Specify the directory containing Word, and select custom installation. **5.** To install the sample templates, turn off the Xs in the check boxes of all the options except Sample Templates. **6.** Click Setup, and insert disks when prompted to do so. **7.** Click OK when the Setup program has finished copying files. ♦

Restoring original templates

If you inadvertently or intentionally alter a template and want to restore the original, you can delete the template and copy the original from the installation disk. The original has the same filename with DT$ as its extension, which means you have to use the Decomp program found on Disk 1 to decompress the file. ♦

Normal template

the document. The default selection is the Normal template, which opens a blank document with the standard menus and Toolbar. Try this to take a look at the other options:

2. Press PgUp until the highlight reaches the template at the top of the Template list box—probably ARTICLE2. Notice the Description area at the bottom of the dialog box, where Word displays a short description of the highlighted template. (This description is the Title information from the template's Summary Info dialog box.)

Template descriptions

3. Press the Down Arrow key to scroll down through the list of templates, reading the description of each one.

As you can tell from their names, the sample templates provide the basis for many common business documents. For example, in Chapter 1 you created a press release while becoming familiar with Word's basic features. You could also have used the sample press-release template supplied with Word, which we'll now take a quick look at.

The Press-Release Template

Assuming that you still have the New dialog box on your screen and that Word's sample templates are available, follow these steps to see the press-release template in action:

Opening a press release

1. Move the highlight to PRESS in the New dialog box, and click OK. Word opens a new document, moves a highlight around the screen, and displays a dialog box:

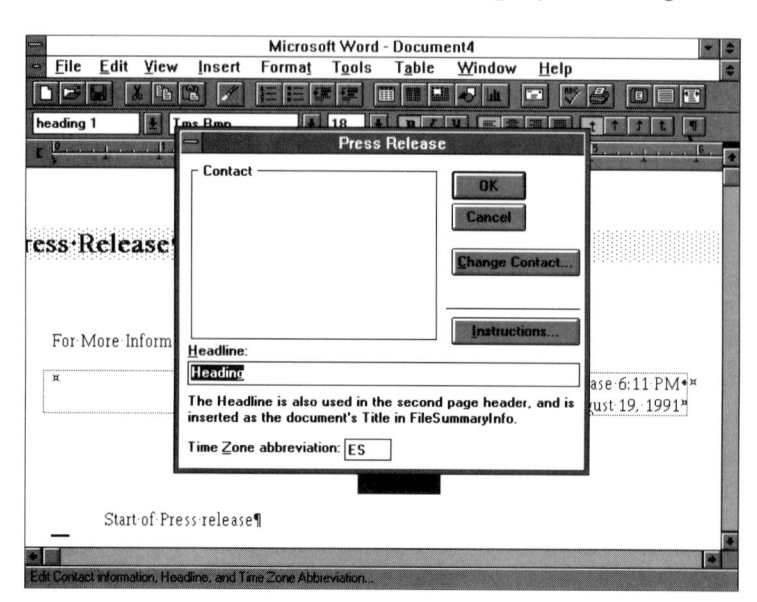

Although this dialog box looks pretty standard, it isn't. It was created specifically for this template by Microsoft, using the Dialog Editor included with Word for Windows version 2.0. (The Dialog Editor program is called MACRODE.EXE; it is located in the WINWORD directory.) The dialog box was displayed by a macro that runs automatically every time you open a new document based on the PRESS template. After you make some entries in the dialog box and click OK, the same macro will gather the information and use it to fill in some of the blanks in the press release.

2. The *Heading* entry in the Headline box should be highlighted (if it isn't, select it). Replace *Heading* with your own press-release title by typing *Extraware Wins Carson Award for "Green" Packaging*—the title from the press release in Chapter 1.

3. Next, click the Change Contact button to display this dialog box:

Changing contact information

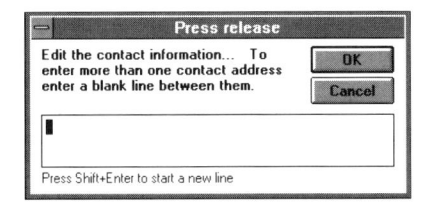

4. Type *Ted Lee*, press Shift-Enter to start a new line, and type *(206) 555-6789*.

5. Click OK to close this dialog box, and click No in the next dialog box you see.

6. The only information left to change is the time zone (unless you live in the Eastern Standard time zone). Highlight ES in the Time Zone box, enter your time zone, and then click OK to close the dialog box.

Specifying time zone

Now watch the screen as Word enters the information from the dialog box in the appropriate places and moves the insertion point to the end of the document. The result is shown on the next page.

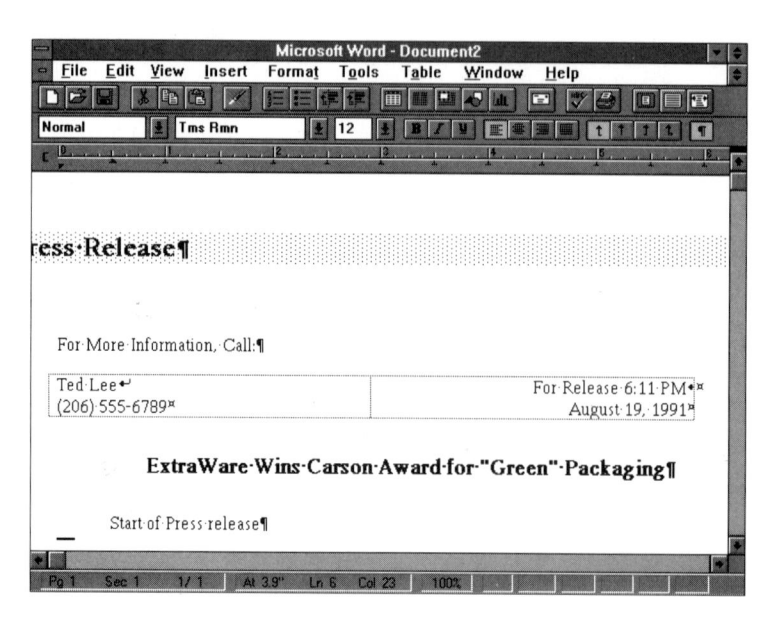

If you actually wanted to create a press release, you could now type the contents or copy them from another file and paste them in here.

This is a pretty nifty way to create a press release, but what we want to stress here is that all you were doing was using one of Word's sample templates, which happens to come with a couple of macros. With a little study and experimentation, you could modify this template to create and fill in other types of documents.

The Memo Template

The next template we will look at is used to create a memo, but it goes way beyond merely producing a form for you to fill in. This template, named MEMO2 in the list displayed when you choose New from the File menu, keeps track of the people to whom you normally send memos, allowing you to simply click a name to add it to the distribution list for the current memo. To try this template, follow these steps:

1. Open a new document based on the MEMO2 template. If this is the first time this template has been used since Word was installed, you see a description of the template. Click OK to close this dialog box. Word then displays the Distribution List Manager dialog box so that you can build a distribution list.

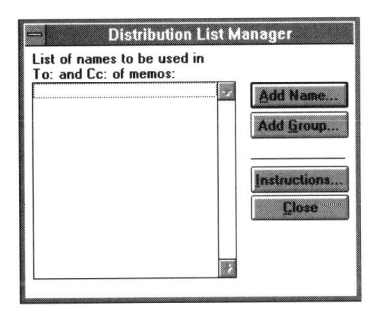

Chapter 6 More Reusable Documents: Using Word's Templates 123

2. Click the Add Name button to display this dialog box: *Adding names*

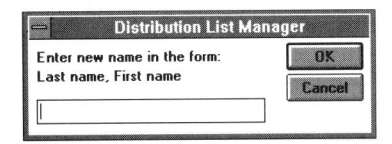

3. Follow the directions to add a few names to the list. Then click the Add Group button, and use the dialog boxes Word displays to add a marketing department with two or three people in it. *Adding groups*

4. When you have a few names on your list, click the Close button to move on. Click OK in the next informational dialog box and Yes in the following one. Your screen then looks like the one shown on the following page.

Editing the distribution list	Lazy macro?	Fax cover sheet
You don't have to enter everyone you will ever want to send a memo to. The template has added a few commands to the bottom of the Format menu that you can use to edit this list and take care of other memo-related tasks. To edit the list, choose Manage Distribution List, and use the Add Name and Add Group buttons as you did for the example. ♦	When you open a new document based on a template, you are prompted for information by the macro included in the template. When you open the template itself, the macro doesn't run, so you are not prompted for information. ♦	Another template you might find yourself using frequently is FAX.DOT, which produces a facsimile cover sheet. Each time you open a document based on this template, you fill in the recipient's name, company, phone number, and fax number. When you click the Defaults button, Word fills in another set of text boxes with your information. ♦

[Screenshot: Microsoft Word window showing an InterOffice Memo template with a "To:" dialog box displaying "Address Memo to" list containing Child, Greg; Marketing; Oberlin, Salley; Ropiequet, Suzanne, with Select and Cancel buttons, and Manage Distribution List and Instructions buttons below.]

In the future, you will see this screen whenever you open a document based on this template. The word *Recipient* is highlighted, and your distribution list is poised and ready for you to select a name.

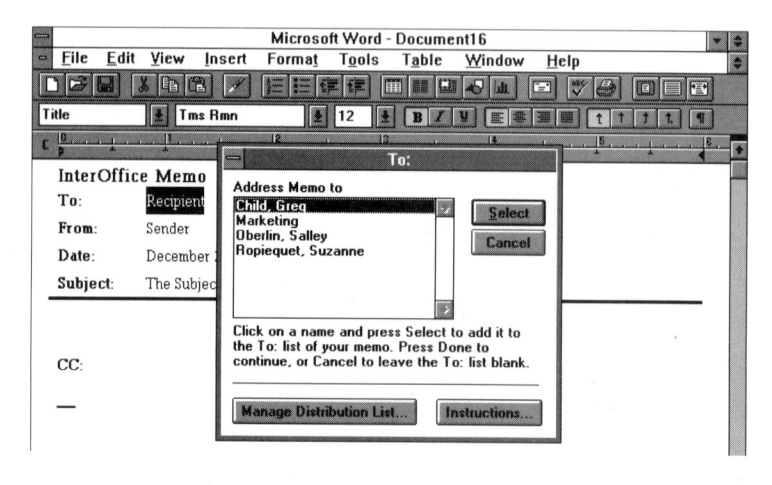

Selecting recipients

5. Select a recipient's name, and click Select. An arrow appears next to the person or group's name, and a button labeled Done appears in the dialog box. (You can select existing names or groups as recipients, or you can click Manage Distribution List to add other names to the list so that you can then select them.)
6. Click the Done button. The word *Recipient* is replaced by the names you have selected. (Selecting a group designates all the people in the group as recipients.)
7. Word moves the highlight to *Sender* and displays a dialog box asking for the name of the memo's sender.

This is enough of a guided tour to give you a good idea of what can be done by adding a macro to a template. Go ahead and continue working with this template on your own, responding to the prompts as they appear. When you finish filling in the memo, you can save it or print it in the usual manner.

Modifying Templates

As mentioned in Chapter 5, the templates that serve as patterns for new documents are stored in the WINWORD directory with DOT extensions. If you want to make a blanket change to the appearance of all new documents patterned on a particular template, you can open the template itself and make the changes there. If you want to change a macro that is part of a template, you can make the changes in the template itself or in any document you have created based on the template. If you make the changes in a document, you are given the option of passing them on to the underlying template so that they will be available to future documents based on that template.

Changing Appearance

As you've seen, if you open a new document based on a template and then fill in the blanks—with or without the prompting of a macro—you end up with a unique document that can be saved without affecting the original template. You can edit that document, changing both the information you have entered and the information supplied by the template, without changing the form of the next new document you open based on the same template. If, however, you open the template itself and make changes, the changes will be reflected in all future documents you open based on that template. To try this out, follow these steps:

1. Choose Open from the File menu to display the Open dialog box:

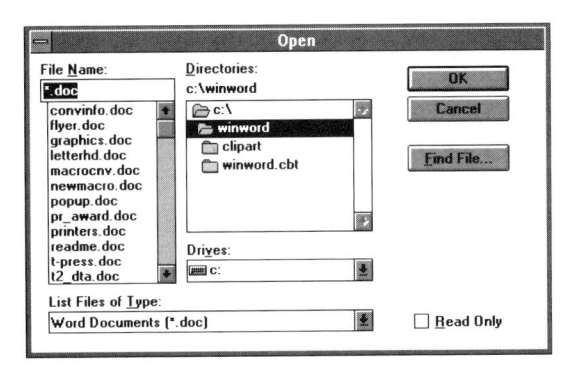

2. Click the down arrow next to the List Files Of Type box to display a list of the standard file types, and then select Document Templates (*.dot).
3. Locate the directory containing the DOT files (probably C:\WINWORD) and open the PRESS template.
4. Templates often contain fields that are replaced by specific information, such as the date or a glossary entry, when a document is opened or printed. To be sure that you don't inadvertantly delete a field, open

Preserving fields

the View menu, and choose Field Codes if it doesn't already have a check mark in front of it.

5. Choose the Zoom command on the View menu to scale the page to 75 percent of the original document size. You can then see the entire PRESS template, like this:

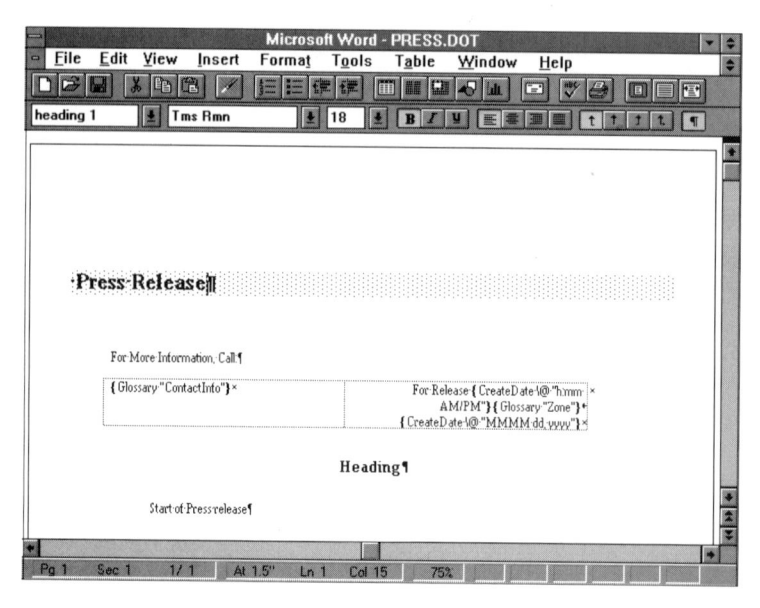

Now make a change to the template. For example, follow these steps to remove the shading from the title and instead enclose it in a shadowed border:

1. Click an insertion point anywhere in the *Press Release* title, and choose Border from the Format menu.
2. Click the Shading button in the Border Paragraphs dialog box to display this dialog box:

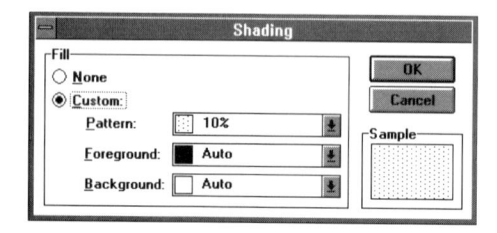

3. Click None, and then click OK to remove the shading from the title.
4. When you return to the Border Paragraphs dialog box, select Shadow in the Preset section, and select the first double line in the Line section. Specify *8 pt* in the From Text box to move the border away from the text a bit. The dialog box should now look like this:

Adding a shadowed border

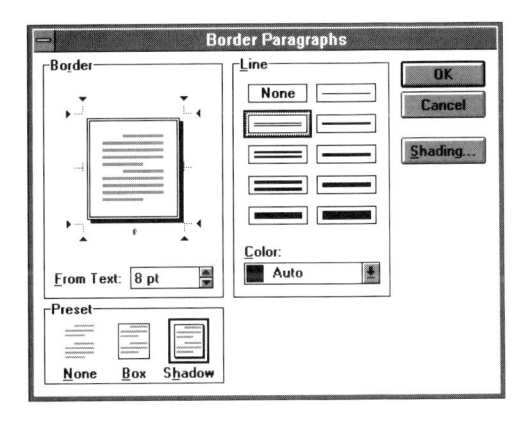

Chapter 6 More Reusable Documents: Using Word's Templates

5. Click OK.
6. Choose Save As from the File menu, and save the template with a new name—for example, you might use PRESS2.DOT.

When you save the template, the modifications you made are saved with it. If you now choose New from the File menu and create a new document based on the modified template, the document produced will reflect the format changes you made but will still include the original macros that prompt you for information.

Changing Macros

As we said earlier, we don't intend to teach you macros in this book. However, we will show you what the macro language looks like and give a quick demonstration of how you might modify a template's macro, using the press-release template as an example.

As you saw earlier, after you supply a contact name and a title for the press release, Word inserts this information in the new press-release document and then leaves the insertion point at the end of the *Start of Press Release* line. If you don't want to include the phrase *Start of Press Release* in your press release, you have to delete it before typing your text. It would be more convenient if Word selected the phrase so that it is automatically deleted when you start typing.

Before we run through the process of modifying the macro to select the phrase, select it manually to give yourself an idea of the steps involved. You can make the selection in several ways. Try the technique on the following page.

1. With the insertion point anywhere in the *Start of Press Release* line, press F8 to turn on Extend-Selection mode.
2. Press F8 two more times to select the entire line.
3. Press Esc to turn off Extend-Selection mode.

The following steps explain how to change the macro to have it automatically select the last line. As we said earlier, this example is not intended to teach you much about macros, but simply to give you a closer look at one while doing some useful work. Don't worry if you don't understand all the ins and outs of this procedure; in fact, feel free to skip it if you have no interest. If you decide you would like to learn more about macros, however, a good place to start is reading those written by the experts, changing them in small ways, and running them to see the effects. Let's get going:

1. With a document based on the PRESS template open on your screen, choose Macro from the Tools menu. Word displays this dialog box:

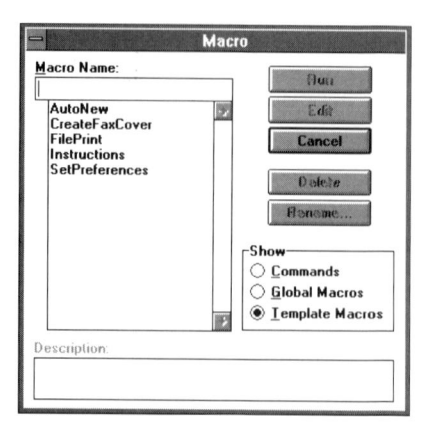

Word's AutoNew macro

The dialog box lists the macros that the folks at Microsoft have included in this template. (If Template Macros is not selected in the Show section, select it.) The macro that Word runs when you create a new document based on the PRESS template is called AutoNew (because it is run automatically when this option is selected from the New dialog box).

Editing a macro

2. Highlight AutoNew in the Macro list box, and then click the Edit button. Word opens the macro in a

special window designed specifically for editing and testing macros, like this:

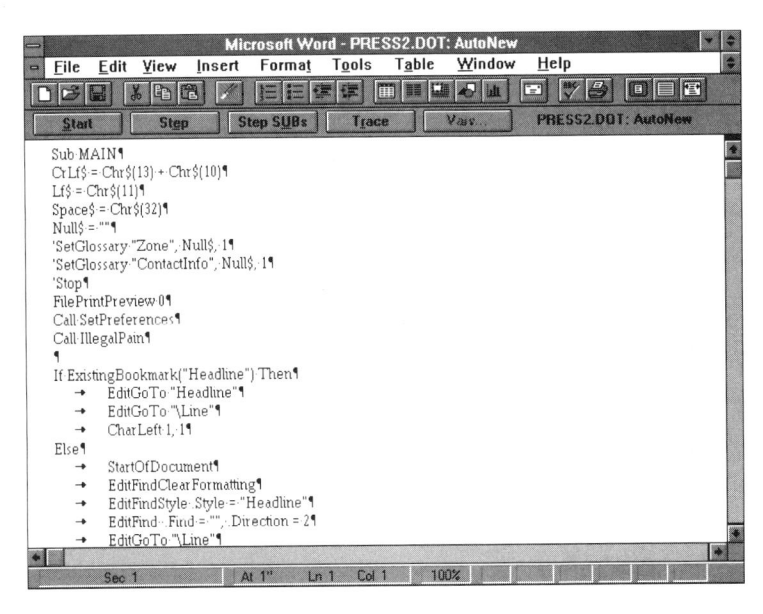

```
Sub MAIN
CrLf$ = Chr$(13) + Chr$(10)
Lf$ = Chr$(11)
Space$ = Chr$(32)
Null$ = ""
'SetGlossary "Zone", Null$, 1
'SetGlossary "ContactInfo", Null$, 1
'Stop
FilePrintPreview 0
Call SetPreferences
Call IllegalPain

If ExistingBookmark("Headline") Then
    EditGoTo "Headline"
    EditGoTo "\Line"
    CharLeft 1, 1
Else
    StartOfDocument
    EditFindClearFormatting
    EditFindStyle Style = "Headline"
    EditFind Find = "", Direction = 2
    EditGoTo "\Line"
```

If you have programmed in other languages, the structure of WordBasic will look familiar. Even if you haven't programmed before, you might be able to figure out what parts of the macro do. Most of the commands in the macro correspond directly to commands you can choose from menus. For example, EditGoTo is the macro equivalent of choosing GoTo from the Edit menu. If choosing a command produces a dialog box, the options in the dialog box are represented by numbers or text following the command.

3. To select the desired phrase in the press release, we need to find the section of the macro that positions the insertion point after inserting custom information in the press-release document. The insertion point is positioned after a predefined "bookmark," or placeholder, called StartOfRelease that has been assigned to the phrase *Start of Press Release*. To find the correct section, choose Find from the Edit menu, then type *StartOfRelease* as the Find What text, and click Find Next. When Word finds the text, the screen looks like the one shown on the next page.

Searching a macro

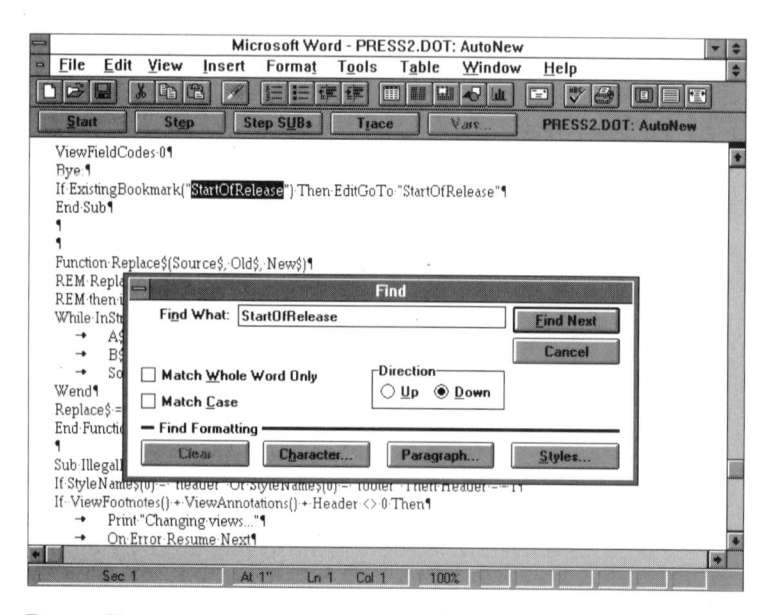

4. Press Esc to close the Find dialog box. The line containing the highlighted term means exactly what you might think: If the StartOfRelease bookmark exists, Word is to go to its location in the document. This is the command responsible for moving the insertion point to the phrase *Start of Press Release*. The next line, End Sub, is the end of this part of the macro—the point at which the press-release document is turned over to you so that you can enter the actual text. To select the phrase, you will have to put some commands between the one containing the highlight and End Sub.
5. Press End, and then press Enter to insert a new line.
6. When you selected the phrase manually, the first step was to turn on Extend-Selection mode. You do that in a macro by entering the command ExtendSelection, which is the macro equivalent of pressing F8. Type *ExtendSelection* now, and then press Enter to start a new line.
7. Add two more ExtendSelection commands, each on its own line.
8. The last step is to turn off Extend-Selection mode, which you do with the Cancel command. Type *Cancel*. The modified part of the macro now looks like this:

Entering commands in macros

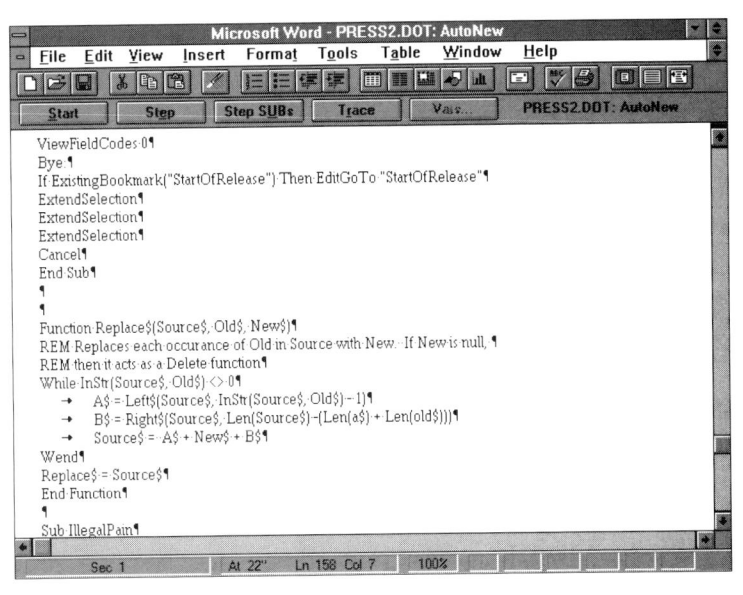

Chapter 6 More Reusable Documents: Using Word's Templates

```
ViewFieldCodes 0
Bye
If ExistingBookmark("StartOfRelease") Then EditGoTo "StartOfRelease"
ExtendSelection
ExtendSelection
ExtendSelection
Cancel
End Sub

Function Replace$(Source$, Old$, New$)
REM Replaces each occurance of Old in Source with New.  If New is null,
REM then it acts as a Delete function
While InStr(Source$, Old$) <> 0
    A$ = Left$(Source$, InStr(Source$, Old$) - 1)
    B$ = Right$(Source$, Len(Source$) - (Len(a$) + Len(old$)))
    Source$ = A$ + New$ + B$
Wend
Replace$ = Source$
End Function

Sub IllegalPain
```

9. Choose Close from the File menu, and answer Yes to the two prompts.

Now put your new macro through its paces by choosing New from the File menu, selecting the PRESS template, and clicking OK. Enter a title for the new press release, click OK again, and watch the screen to see whether Word selects *Start of Press Release*.

That's it for our template appetizer. We encourage you to explore more on your own. Open a document based on each of the templates included with Word. Try out the options, click the buttons, see what happens. You can't hurt your computer or destroy anything, so play a little. Try printing the macros associated with different templates and follow them on paper as they run on your machine. Even if you've never written any kind of program, you will gradually understand the concepts behind macros and will gain an appreciation of the power they can add to Word for Windows.

For more information on specific WordBasic commands, choose Help Index from the Help menu, and then select WordBasic Programming Language from the Reference Information list.

7

Print Merge: Creating Form Documents and Labels

What Is Print Merge?   134
Creating a Form Letter   136
   Creating the Data Document   137
   Completing the Main Document   139
   Merging the Documents   141
Creating a More Sophisticated Letter   143
   Adding Fields to the Data Document   143
   Editing the Main Document   144
Using the MAILLABL Template   146

Fields
Page 135

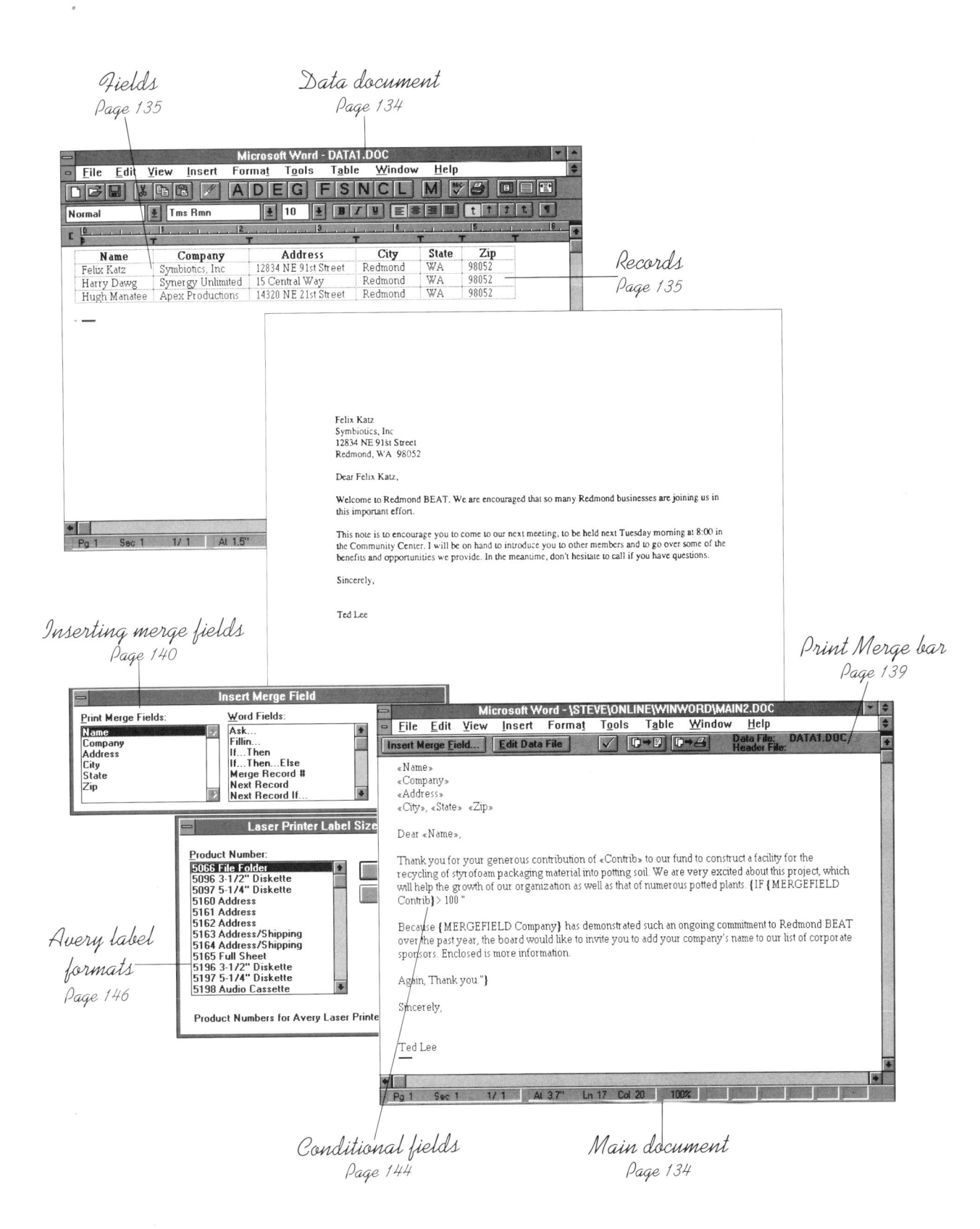

Data document
Page 134

Records
Page 135

Inserting merge fields
Page 140

Print Merge bar
Page 139

Avery label formats
Page 146

Conditional fields
Page 144

Main document
Page 134

Most people over the age of 18 in the United States have received at least a few personalized form letters. You probably get them fairly often. You know the sort of thing—your name is sprinkled liberally throughout, with a few references to the city in which you live or some other item of personal information. Mail of this sort is an example of the use, and often the abuse, of the print-merge feature of a word-processing program. We certainly don't want to assist in the destruction of the forests of the world by showing you how to send junk mail to millions of people. But if you'll use your new knowledge wisely and with restraint, we'll introduce you to the mysteries of Word for Window's Print Merge command.

Actually, starting with Word for Windows 2.0, print merge isn't even all that mysterious. If you have used this feature in other word processors or in previous versions of Word, you will be pleasantly surprised at the ease with which you can now create print-merge documents using Word for Windows. If you have never used print merge (or mail merge, as it is often called), then a definition may be in order.

What Is Print Merge?

Print merge, as its name implies, is the printing of a bunch of similar documents by merging the information in one document, called the main document, with what is essentially a database of variable information in a second document, called the data document.

Main document →
The main document contains the information that does not change from document to document—the text of a form letter, for example—along with placeholders called merge fields for the variable information and codes that control the merging process. A document with a typical set of codes is shown at the top of the next page.

Data document →
Each of the words enclosed in chevrons is a name that matches the name of a field in the corresponding data document, also shown on the next page. As you can see, the data document contains the information that changes with each printed document: name, address, city, and so on. The data in this particular document is stored in a Word table, but there

Chapter 7 Print Merge: Creating Form Documents and Labels

Merge fields

«fName» «lName»
«Address»
«City», «State» «Zip»

Dear «fName»,

   Thank you for your order of «Num» copies of our book "«Title»."

Fields   *Header*

fName	lName	Address	City	State	Zip	Num	Title
Bernard	Namberry	124 Main Street	Seattle	WA	98155	5	A Quick Course in Word for Windows
Judy	Johnson	687 S. 178th Ave	Kirkland	WA	98033	2	A Quick Course in Windows

Records

Records
Fields
Headers

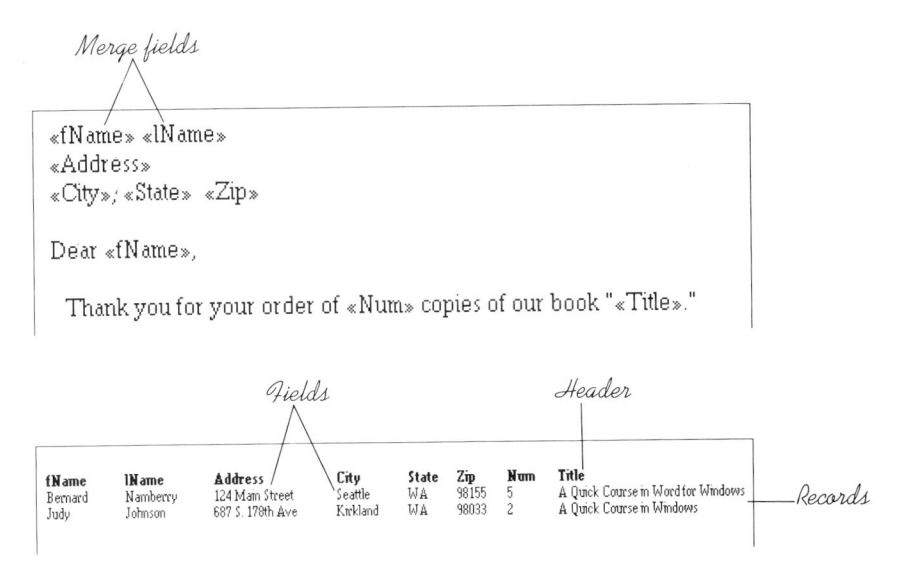

are other formats available. (Called tab-delimited or comma-delimited fields, these formats are standard output formats for most spreadsheets and databases.) Each row in the table, which is called a record, contains the variable information for one printed document. Each cell (the intersection of a column and a row), which is called a field, contains one variable item—usually a single word or a short phrase. The first record (the top row of the table) is called the header. Each field in the header contains a field name that identifies the contents of the column beneath it.

You can include as many records as you want (or as many as disk space permits) in a data document. Using this table format, you can have up to 31 fields per record. (With other formats, the number of fields is practically unlimited.)

The result of merging the example main document and data document would be two letters, one addressed to Bernard Namberry and the other to Judy Johnson, each with the appropriate information instead of the merge fields.

Although print-merge documents can be pretty complex—including mathematical calculations, logical comparisons, and branching instructions—this simple example is as complex as most get. In addition to creating letters, print merge is a handy tool for filling in forms and is particularly useful when the information needed to fill in the forms is already included in a database or spreadsheet. For example, you might use print merge to print invoices, checks, and insurance forms, as well as all kinds of labels—for mailings and for collections of disks, audio cassettes, CDs, video tapes, comic books, or books. Printing labels of various types is such a common use of print merge that Microsoft has included a template with Word for Windows to guide you through the process. We'll have a look at that template in a moment. Right now, let's create a simple form letter.

Creating a Form Letter

The first stage of creating a form letter is to take a few moments to plan it. You might draft a sample letter and mark all the words or phrases that will vary from letter to letter. Then you might organize your sources of information to make sure you have easy access to all the names, addresses, and other tidbits of information required. Only after these tasks have been completed will you actually create the main document and data document. Assume that we have already taken care of this planning stage for you so that you can now start the interesting part.

1. Click the New button to open a new document. (In actual practice, you might base this document on a letterhead template or some other template, but for this example, the document can be based on the default Normal template.)
2. Click the Save button, and in the Save As dialog box, assign the name Main1 to the file and click OK. Fill out the Summary Info dialog box, and click OK again.
3. Choose Print Merge from the File menu to display this dialog box:

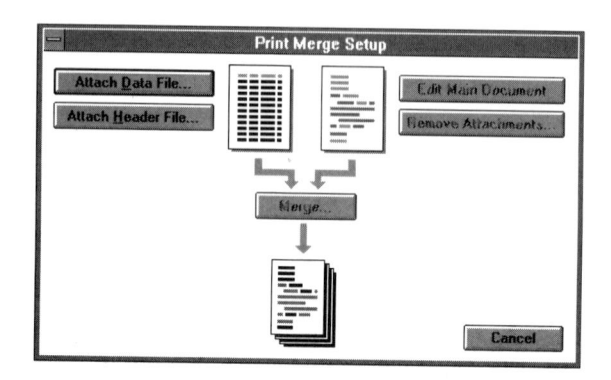

As you can see, Word graphically displays the print-merge process and offers you a few options. The default selection is Attach Data File.

Creating the Data Document

With most word processors, you need to create the data document before you begin the print-merge process. Not so with Word for Windows, as you'll soon see:

1. Press Enter to accept the default selection. Word displays this dialog box to allow you to select the desired data document:

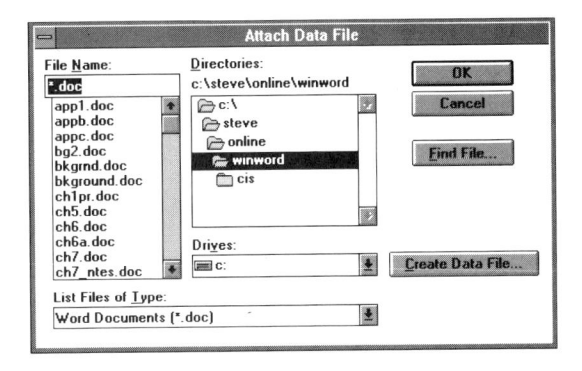

2. Because you have not yet created the data document, click the Create Data File button. Word displays yet another dialog box so that you can enter the names of all the data-document fields:

    Creating a data document

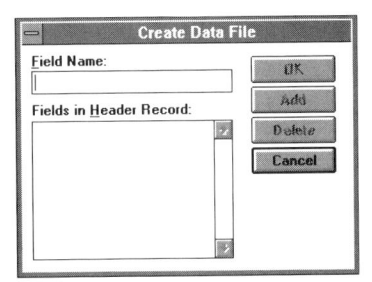

3. To enter the first field name, type *Name*, and click the Add button or press Enter.

    Entering fields

4. Repeat this process for each of these names: Company, Address, City, State, Zip. The result is shown on the next page.

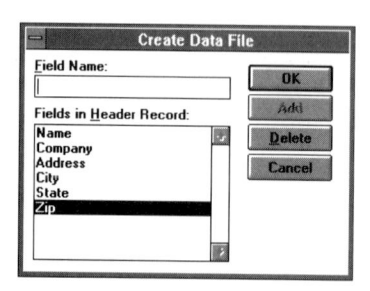

Correcting errors → If you make a mistake, move the highlight to the error, click the Delete button, and redo the field name.

5. When you have entered all the field names, click OK to close the dialog box. Word returns you to the previous dialog box, where you can name and save the data document. Type *data1* as the name, and click OK. Word then opens this data document:

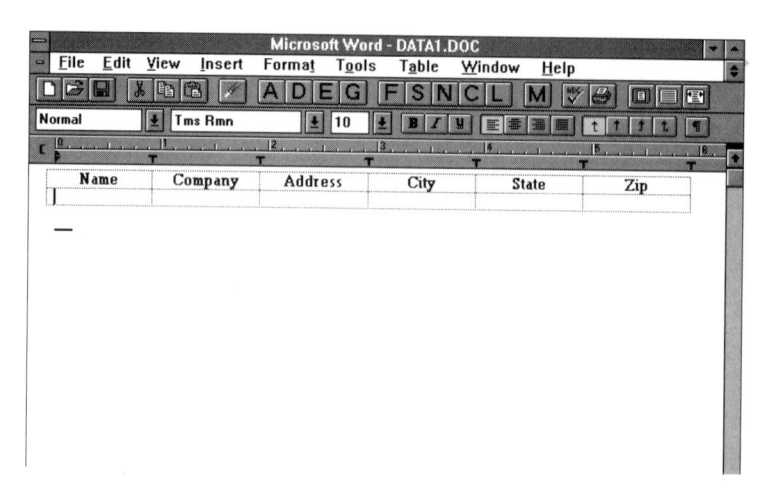

Field location

The location of the fields in the data document is not important to the operation of the Print Merge command. The main document can use any combination of fields in any order. If the order of fields is significant to you, you can insert them manually or move them after they have been inserted with the F button on the Toolbar. ♦

Missing buttons

Word removes the ten Toolbar buttons that you are least likely to need when working with a print-merge data document, replacing them with buttons for print-merge tasks. You can choose menu commands to perform the tasks associated with all of the removed buttons except Envelope. ♦

Button descriptions

Place the mouse pointer over any of the buttons on the Toolbar, hold down the left mouse button, and look at the status bar, where the purpose of the button is displayed. Then move the pointer away from the Toolbar before releasing the mouse button, so as not to choose the Toolbar button's command. ♦

Chapter 7 Print Merge: Creating Form Documents and Labels 139

The data document is based on the DATAFILE template. Notice that after the document is loaded, the Toolbar includes a series of lettered buttons, each representing a command. We'll take a closer look at these buttons later.

Notice also that Word has automatically inserted a table in the document with the field names you specified in the top header row. The names identify the type of information that will be contained in the columns below.

When you print-merge the letter, each copy will use the information from one record, or row, in the data-document table. So your next task is to enter a few records. You can enter any names and addresses you would like. Here are the ones we use for the example:

Entering records

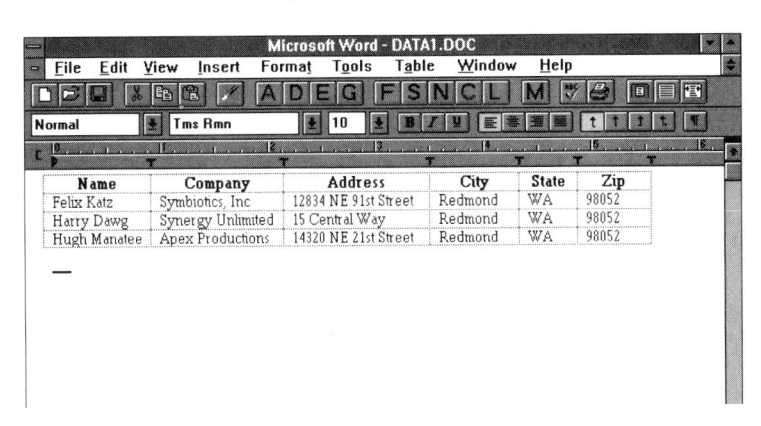

1. With the insertion point in the first column of the second row, type the first name, press Tab to jump to the next column, enter the company, press Tab, and so on until you have entered the information for the last column in the row. Then press Tab again to add a new row and move to the start of the next row.
2. Repeat this process to enter a few more records.
3. Return to the main document by clicking the M button on the Toolbar.

Returning to the main document

Completing the Main Document

When you return to the main document, the most obvious change is the addition of a Print Merge bar between the Ribbon and the Ruler (if they are displayed), as shown on the next page.

Print Merge bar

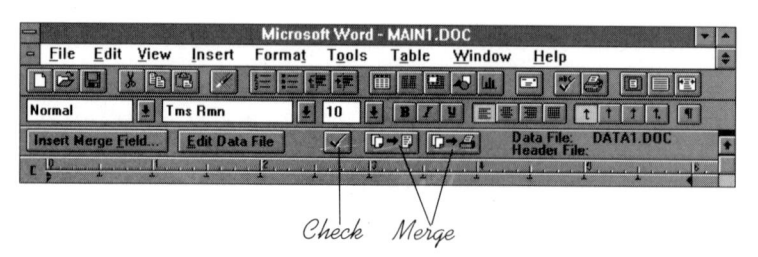

[Screenshot of Microsoft Word - MAIN1.DOC window with toolbar, annotated with "Check" and "Merge" labels pointing to two buttons]

The buttons on this bar provide shortcuts for commands that you might otherwise have to wander through several layers of dialog boxes to get to.

The next task is to type the text of the letter, inserting merge fields for the information that will be drawn from the data document. Let's start by entering the addressee information, which consists almost entirely of merge fields:

Inserting merge fields

1. With the insertion point at the top of the blank document, click the Insert Merge Field button to display this dialog box:

[Insert Merge Field dialog box showing Print Merge Fields list (Name, Company, Address, City, State, Zip) and Word Fields list (Ask..., Fillin..., If...Then, If...Then...Else, Merge Record #, Next Record, Next Record If...) with OK and Cancel buttons]

The left list box displays the fields you defined in the data document.

2. You want to insert the Name field, which is already highlighted, so simply click OK. The dialog box disappears, and the Name merge field appears at the insertion point enclosed in chevrons. (If Word displays {MERGEFIELD Name} instead of Name, choose Field Codes from the View menu to turn off the display of codes. You can then see the code results in your document.) Press Enter to move to the next line.

Turning off field codes

3. Click Insert Merge Field again, insert the Company merge field, and press Enter. Then repeat this procedure for the Address merge field.

4. Click Insert Merge Field, insert City, type a comma and a space, insert State, type two spaces, and insert Zip. The address section now looks like this:

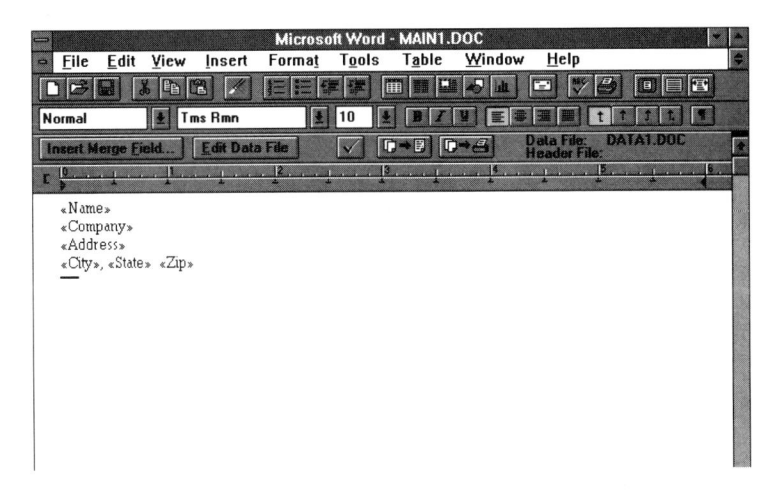

Chapter 7 Print Merge: Creating Form Documents and Labels　　141

5. Press Enter a couple of times, and then type the body of the letter:

   Dear (*click Insert Merge Field, and select Name*):

   Welcome to Redmond BEAT. We are encouraged that so many Redmond businesses are joining us in this important effort.

   This note is to invite you to come to our next meeting, to be held next Tuesday morning at 8:00 in the Community Center. I will be on hand to introduce you to other members and to go over some of the benefits and opportunities we provide. In the meantime, don't hesitate to call if you have questions.

   Sincerely,

   Ted Lee

Merging the Documents

You're now ready to merge the main document with the data document. You have a couple of options here. Notice the three buttons near the center of the Print Merge bar. If you click the one with the check mark in it, your main and data documents are checked for errors. If you click the second button, Word merges the main document with the data document and puts the resulting letters into a new document that you can save and print later. If you click the third button,　　← *Print-merge options*

Checking for errors

Merging to a document

Print-merging

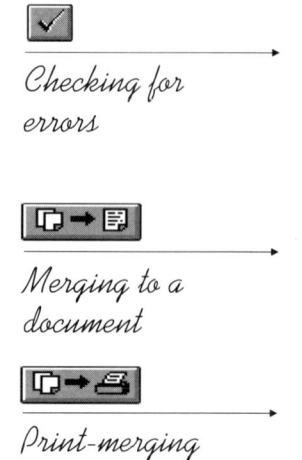

Word merges the documents but sends them directly to the printer.

1. Click the Check button to have Word check your documents. If you followed the directions you should see a dialog box announcing the fact that the documents contain no print-merge errors. If there are errors, they will be pointed out so that you can correct them.
2. Now click the Document Merge button. Word opens a new document window called FormLetters and then "prints" the letters to the document, with a page break between each letter.
3. If your printer is turned on and you want to try the Print Merge button, go ahead and click it. Here are three printed letters:

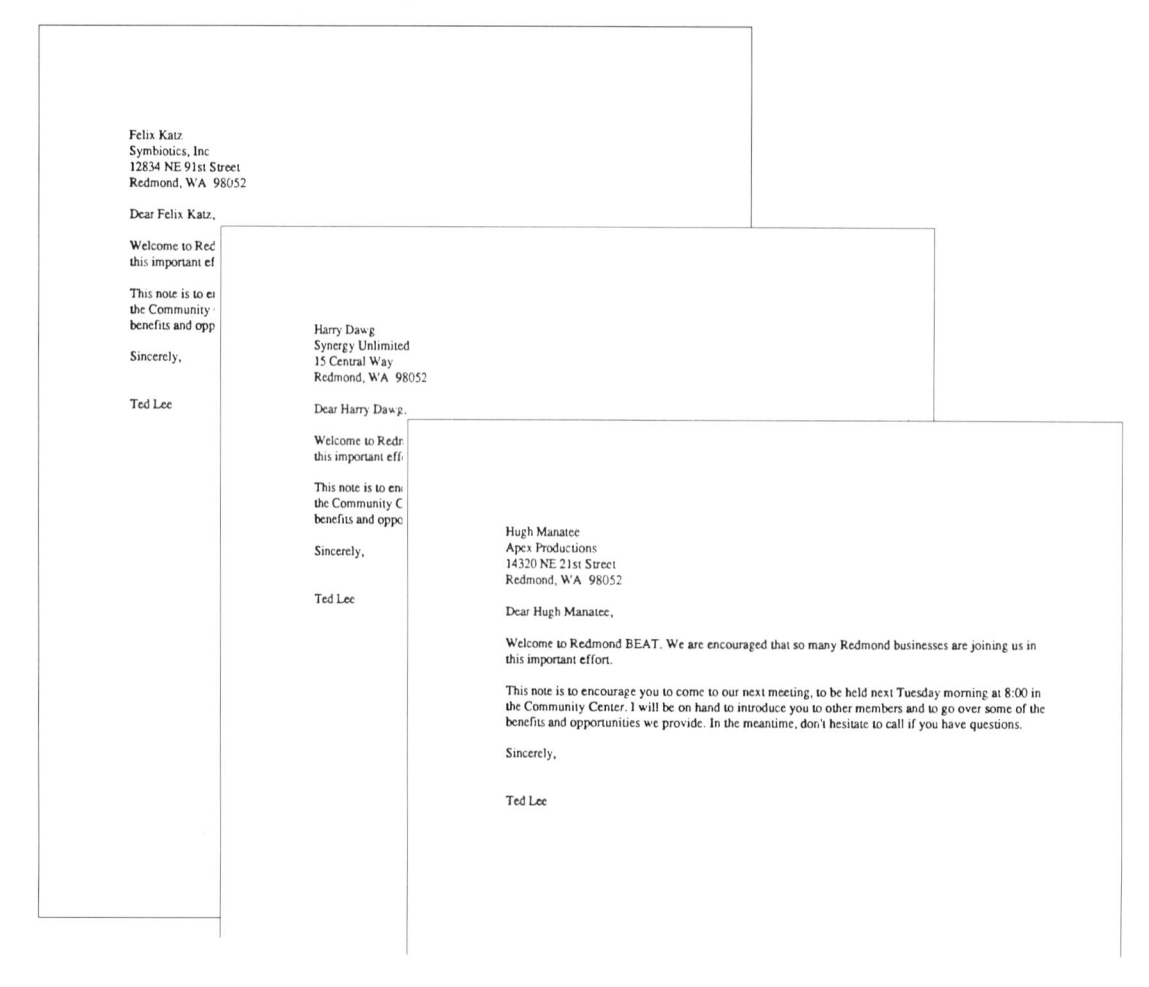

Felix Katz
Symbiotics, Inc
12834 NE 91st Street
Redmond, WA 98052

Dear Felix Katz,

Welcome to Red
this important ef

This note is to e
the Community
benefits and opp

Sincerely,

Ted Lee

Harry Dawg
Synergy Unlimited
15 Central Way
Redmond, WA 98052

Dear Harry Dawg,

Welcome to Redn
this important eff

This note is to en
the Community C
benefits and oppo

Sincerely,

Ted Lee

Hugh Manatee
Apex Productions
14320 NE 21st Street
Redmond, WA 98052

Dear Hugh Manatee,

Welcome to Redmond BEAT. We are encouraged that so many Redmond businesses are joining us in this important effort.

This note is to encourage you to come to our next meeting, to be held next Tuesday morning at 8:00 in the Community Center. I will be on hand to introduce you to other members and to go over some of the benefits and opportunities we provide. In the meantime, don't hesitate to call if you have questions.

Sincerely,

Ted Lee

Now that you know how to do simple print merges, let's look at some more sophisticated print-merge features.

Creating a More Sophisticated Letter

We named the main and data documents for this example MAIN1.DOC and DATA1.DOC, respectively, but we could have saved them with any valid names. And we can open and edit the documents just like any other documents. We can add fields and records to the table in the data document the same way we can add columns and rows to any table. And we can add tables, charts, pictures, and various types of Word fields to the main document. We can even include fields that cause the print-merge process to pause and prompt for additional information that is not included in the data document.

Word gives you several ways to control exactly what is printed in a merged document. Although the process of exercising that control is not incredibly complicated, a complete explanation is beyond the scope of this book. However, we can quickly turn our original form letter into one that makes a conditional decision, just to give you an idea of what can be done.

Let's create a letter thanking people for their contributions to Redmond BEAT, and include a paragraph that Word prints only if the contribution is over a certain amount. To do this, we have to add a field to the data document to hold the amount of the contribution.

Adding Fields to the Data Document

Because the data document is just another Word document, you can switch back to it by choosing it from the list of open documents at the bottom of the Windows menu or using the Open command on the File menu. Then with the data document on your screen, follow these steps:

1. Click the F button on the Toolbar bar to display this dialog box:

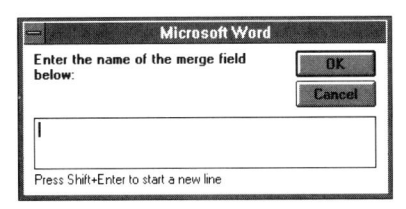

Adding a field

2. Type *Contrib* as the field name, and press Enter. Word adds the field to the right end of the table.
3. Credit each of the people in your data document with a contribution—make one for $50, one for $100, and one for $150.
4. Click the M button to move back to the main document.

Editing the Main Document

To give us a jump start on creating a new main document, we'll edit the one we've already saved.

1. Select the body of MAIN1.DOC (the two paragraphs between the salutation and the closing), and delete it.
2. Now type the text you see here:

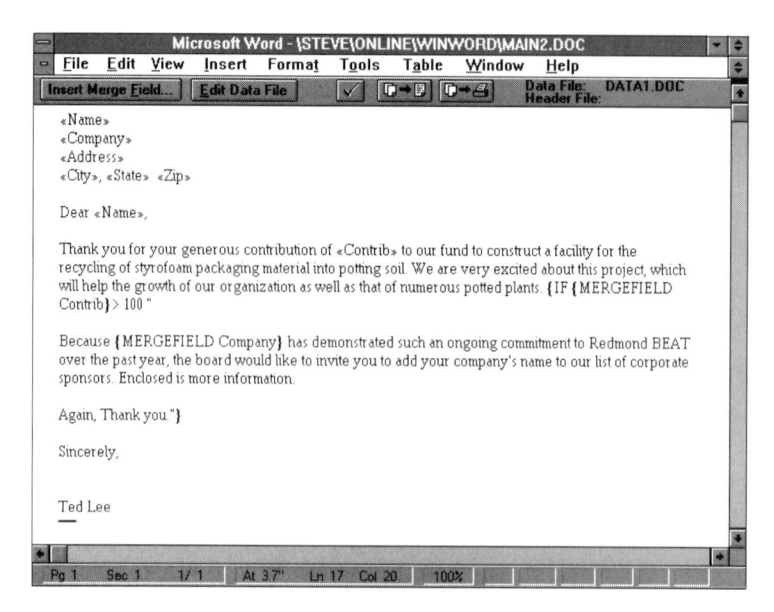

When you get to the contribution, click the Insert Merge Field button, and select the new Contrib field, which Word automatically added to the dialog box.

At the end of the first paragraph is some text that looks like gibberish (starting with {IF). This is a conditional field that causes the next paragraph to be printed if the amount of the contribution is over $100. To insert this conditional field, follow these steps:

Conditional fields

1. With the insertion point at the end of the first paragraph, click Insert Merge Field to display the Insert Merge Field dialog box:

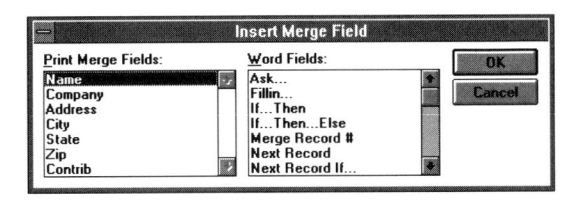

Chapter 7 Print Merge: Creating Form Documents and Labels

2. Select If...Then from the Word Field list box on the right, and press Enter to insert this field in the MAIN1 document:

   {IF Exp Op Exp "TextIfTrue"}

   This is a "pattern" for a field that compares two expressions and inserts some text if the comparison is true. What we want this field to do, in plain English, is tell Word that if the amount of the contribution is greater than $100, Word should print a paragraph offering special thanks. Here's how to adjust the field:

3. Highlight the first Exp, click the Insert Merge Field button, select the Contrib field, and press Enter. Word replaces the highlighted Exp with {MERGEFIELD Contrib} (or Contrib in chevrons if the display of field codes is turned off).

4. Highlight Op, which stands for Operator, and type > (the greater than symbol).

5. Highlight the remaining Exp, and type *100*. The field now looks like this:

   {IF {MERGEFIELD Contrib} > 100 "TextIfTrue"}

Operators	Menu equivalents	Field formats
The allowable operators are: = (equal) < (less than) <= (less than or equal to) > (greater than) >= (greater than or equal to) <>(unequal) ♦	The commands represented by the Check button and the two Merge buttons are also available by choosing Print Merge from the File menu, then choosing Merge from the resulting dialog box. ♦	Inserted fields may appear as {MERGEFIELD *field name*} or as the field name enclosed in chevrons. You can switch between the two formats by highlighting the field and pressing Shift-F9. ♦

6. Highlight TextIfTrue (but not the quotation marks), press Enter twice to start a new paragraph, and then type the text shown in the graphic on page 144, inserting a field for the company name. (Notice that we begin the conditional text with a paragraph break to prevent the printing of a blank line in letters to contributors of less than $100.)
7. That's all there is to it. You can now click the Check button and print-merge the letters to see the results.

If you credited three companies with contributions of $50, $100, and $150, the first two letters won't have the extra paragraph, and the third letter will have it. Try changing the operator in the conditional field from > to >= and then merging again.

For another print-merge example, let's take a look at the template provided by Microsoft for creating labels.

Using the MAILLABL Template

The MAILLABL template provides a quick way to format a main document so that it will print on standard-size labels. As you saw in Chapter 6, templates can include macros that guide you through the process of filling in a form. When you open a new document based on the MAILLABL template, a macro displays a dialog box from which you can select an Avery label format. (Avery is a brand of label available in most office-supply stores. If you don't know which label format you want, you may have to experiment a little to locate the one best suited to your needs.) Let's put this template to work:

1. Choose New from the File menu, select MAILLABL, and click OK to open a new document and display a dialog box similar to this one:

Avery label formats

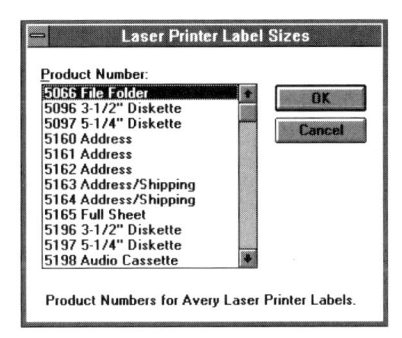

Chapter 7 Print Merge: Creating Form Documents and Labels

The macro that displays this dialog box first checks your system settings and then displays one of several available lists, so your dialog box might not be identical to this one.

2. Select the 5160 Address label if you have this list or the 4143 Address label if you have a different list, click OK, and sit back and watch while Word builds a table to display the number of labels that fit on a page.

    Selecting an address label

3. When Word asks whether you want to print a single label or multiple labels, select Multiple Labels so that you can use print merge.

    Multiple labels

4. When Word asks whether the merge names and the data are located in separate files, answer No. You then see the Attach Data File dialog box shown earlier.

5. Locate and attach DATA1.DOC, the data document you created for the previous example. The macro then presents this dialog box so that you can lay out the main document:

Adding fields to labels

6. Select Name from the list box on the left, press Tab to move to the list box on the right, select the paragraph symbol, and click the Add To Label button. This places Name and a paragraph symbol in the Sample box.
7. Repeat this process with the Company, Address, City, State, and Zip fields (adding a comma and spaces as needed) to create an entire mailing label. Check your work after adding each field. If you make a mistake, simply click the Undo Last Add button, and add that field again.

Removing fields

Completing the main document

8. Once you have set up the sample label, choose Done to have the macro copy the sample to all the labels in the main document. (This takes a minute or so.)
9. Click the Check button, and then click either the Document Merge or Print Merge button to see the results.

Setting up a document to print mailing labels used to take a lot of patience and often wasted a lot of paper with trial-and-error printings. Microsoft's ready-made MAILLABL template takes all the labor out of this task, leaving you free to work on more important projects.

Index

4143 Address label 147
5160 Address label 147
? wildcard 46
¶ button 15, 91

A

adding
    fields to data document 143
    styles to templates 73
    text to outlines 33
adjusting
    column widths 104
    header/footer position 114
    indents 78
    margins 24, 78, 104
    outline levels 32
    size of charts 96
aligning charts 97
Alt key 12
applying styles 70, 74
    as you type 75
    from keyboard 73
Arrange All command 20
arranging windows 20
AutoNew macro 128

B

Back button (Help) 26
backgrounders, creating 30
Bar command (Chart) 95
Body Text button (Outline) 34
Bold button 8–9, 92, 105, 112
bookmarks 129
Border command 62, 93, 96, 105, 112, 126
borders, shadowed 126
boxes
    drawing 62
    putting around charts 96
    Ribbon
        Font 8
        Size 73
        Style 56, 69, 71, 77
    shadowed 126
Break command 113
breaks
    page 113
    section 67
Browse Backward button (Help) 26
Browse Forward button (Help) 26
browsing in Help 26
Bullets And Numbering command 35
buttons
    Header and Footer 111
    Help
        Back 26
        Browse Backward 26
        Browse Forward 26
        Go To 27
        Search 26
    Maximize 3, 21

Outline
    Body Text 34
    Collapse 36
    Demote 32, 36
    Expand 36
    Promote 32, 34
    Show 1 35
    Show 2 35
    Show All 35
Print Merge
    Check 142, 146, 148
    Document Merge 142, 148
    F 138, 143
    Insert Merge Field 140, 144–145
    M 139, 144
    Print Merge 142, 148
Print Preview
    Margins 24, 114
    One Page 24
    Print 24
    Two Pages 24, 113
Ribbon
    ¶ 15, 91
    Bold 8–9, 92, 105, 112
    Center 11, 61, 73, 92
    Decimal Tab 93
    Italic 9, 61
    Justify 11, 73
    Right Align 11
    Underline 61
Toolbar
    Chart 94
    Columns 65
    Copy 42
    Cut 77, 89, 109
    New 19, 77, 87, 107, 136
    Normal View 33, 36, 69
    Numbered List 68, 78
    Open 18, 60
    Paste 42, 77, 89
    Print 24, 108
    Save 16, 18, 33, 61, 87, 94, 105, 108, 136
    Table 87, 90, 94, 103
    Undo 44

C

cells, joining 91
Center button 11, 61, 73, 92
centering text 73
changing
    appearance of templates 125
    chart title 96
    column width 89
    data series 95
    direction of search 46
    font 8, 61
    function of templates 127
    glossary-entry codes 40
    graphic size 84
    gridlines 93
    macros 127
    number of print copies 25
    row height 91
    size 8–9, 61
    styles 73
    summary information 60
    templates 124
Character command 7, 61

character formats 7
characters, nonprinting 8, 15
Chart button 94
charts
    adjusting size of 96
    aligning 97
    changing title 96
    creating 94
    moving legends 96
    pasting into document 96
    putting box around 96
Check button (Print Merge) 142, 146, 148
checking
    grammar 52
    spelling 49
chevrons 134, 140
choosing commands 12
    with keyboard 12
clearing contents of tables 90
clicking 4
Clipboard 42–43, 77
    contents of 43
    vs. glossary 37
Close command (Control menu) 22
Close command (File menu) 22, 107, 109, 131
closed spacing 16
closing
    documents 22, 109
    Help screen 27
    Print Preview 24
    window panes 22
Collapse button (Outline) 36
collapsing outlines 35
column markers 90
Column Width command 105
columns
    adjusting width of 89, 104
    deleting 90
    formatting 65
    moving 89
Columns button 65
Columns command 65–66
comma-delimited fields 135
commands
    Arrange All 20
    Bar (Chart) 95
    Border 62, 93, 96, 105, 112, 126
    Break 113
    Bullets And Numbering 35
    Character 7, 61
    choosing 12
    choosing with keyboard 12
    Close (Control menu) 22
    Close (File menu) 22, 107, 109, 131
    Column Width 105
    Columns 65–66
    Convert Table To Text 94
    Convert Text To Table 94
    Copy 13, 42
    Cut 13, 43
    Delete Columns 90
    Delete Rows 90
    Draft 13, 32
    Exit 27, 41

commands *(continued)*
    Exit (Help) 27
    Exit And Return To *filename*
        (Chart) 96
    Field Codes 112, 126, 140
    File 60, 98, 107
    Find 45–46, 75, 129
    Find File 57
    Footnote 64, 67
    Frame 83
    Glossary 37, 39–40
    Grammar 52
    Gridlines 104
    Header/Footer 109–110
    Help Index 16, 26, 131
    Help Keyboard 16
    Hyphenation 79
    Insert Rows 91
    Links 98
    Macro 128–129
    Manage Distribution List 124
    Merge Cells 91
    New 106–107, 119, 131, 146
    New Window 21
    Open 125
    Options 14, 69, 75
    Outline 31, 33
    Page Layout 67, 83, 94
    Page Setup 23, 78, 104
    Paragraph 7, 72, 78–79, 97,
        104–105
    Paste 13, 42–43
    Paste Cells 110
    Paste Special 98
    Picture 83, 85, 87
    Print 25, 27
    Print Merge 136, 138
    Print Preview 24, 65, 67, 113
    Print Setup 23, 78
    repeating 75
    Replace 47, 75
    Ribbon 2, 13
    Row Height 91
    Ruler 2, 14
    Save As 16, 18, 60, 106, 127
    Select Table 90, 93–94, 109
    Series In Columns (Chart) 95
    Spelling 49–51
    Style 73, 76
    Toolbar 2, 13
comparing expressions in
    print merge 145
conditional
    merge fields 144
    decisions in print merge 143
context-sensitive help 27
controlling print merge 143
conventions
    glossary-entry 39
    keys 4
Convert Table To Text command 94
Convert Text To Table command 94
Copy button 42
Copy command 13, 42
copying
    styles 77
    text 42

with drag-and-drop 43
correcting misspellings 50
creating
    charts 94
    data documents 137
    form letters 136
    frames 82
    memos with template 122
    new documents 19, 136
    press releases with template 120
    styles 71
    tables 87
cropping graphics 86
custom
    dialog boxes 118, 121
    dictionaries 49, 51
    styles 71
customizing display 13–14
Cut button 77, 89, 109
Cut command 13, 43

D

data documents 134
    adding fields to 143
    creating 137
DATAFILE template 139
dates, inserting 111
Date button 111
Decimal Tab button 93
decimal-aligning in tables 92
Decomp program 119
decompressing files 119
default styles 70
defining styles 72
Delete Columns command 90
Delete Rows command 90
deleting
    glossary entries 40
    headings from outline 35
    rows or columns 90
    text 43
    without using Clipboard 44
Demote button (Outline) 32, 36
dialog boxes 13
    custom 118, 121
Dialog Editor 121
dictionaries
    custom 49, 51
    Main 49
directories, switching 19
display, customizing 13–14
displaying
    Ribbon 2
    Ruler 2
    status bar 15
    style area 69, 75
    Toolbar 2
DOC extension 16, 59
Document Merge button (Print
    Merge) 142, 148
document window 2
documents
    closing 22, 109
    creating new 19, 136
    editing 41
    expanding 21
    grammar-checking 52
    hyphenating 79

merging 60, 107
    graphics into 82
moving around 4
opening 18
    existing 42
preserving previous version 18
previewing 24
print merging 141
printing 22
saving
    as templates 106, 115
    existing 18
    new 16
selecting 6, 16
spell-checking 49
working with multiple 20
DOT extension 124
double-clicking 4
    setting speed of 4
Draft command 13, 32
Draft view 32
drag-and-drop
    copying with 43
    moving with 43
    in outlines 36
dragging 5–6, 9
drawing
    boxes 62
    lines 62, 112
DT$ extension 119

E

editing
    documents 41
        print-merge 144
    undoing 44
ellipsis (...) 13
entering records 139
Excel 98
Exit And Return To *filename*
    command (Chart) 96
Exit command 27, 41
Exit command (Help) 27
Expand button (Outline) 36
expanding
    documents 21
    outlines 35
    windows 3
Extend-Selection mode 6
    macro equivalent 130
    turning on and off 7, 42, 128
extending selection 6
extensions
    DOC 16, 59
    DOT 124
    DT$ 119
    WMF 82

F

F button (Print Merge) 138, 143
field codes, turning on 112, 126, 140
Field Codes command 112, 126, 140
fields 111, 125
    adding to data document 143
    comma-delimited 135
    merge 134, 135
    tab-delimited 135
File command 60, 98, 107

Index

files
  decompressing 119
  finding 57
  naming 16
  statistics about 17
Find command 45–46, 75, 129
Find File command 57
finding
  files 57
  keyboard shortcut for 45, 47
  special characters 46
  specific case 46
  styles 75
  text 44
    using wildcards 46
  whole words 46
font, changing 8, 61
Font box 8
Footer window 110
footers 108
  adjusting position of 114
  formatting 112
  selecting 112
  viewing 113
Footnote command 64, 67
footnotes 63
  formatting 63
  positioning 67
Footnotes window 64
form letters 134
formats
  bold 8–9
  character 7
  italic 9
  multicolumn 65
  paragraph 7
  reflected in Ribbon 10
formatting 61
  and glossary entries 39
  boxes 62
  footers 112
  footnotes 63
  letterheads 104
  lists 68
  sections 65
  shading 63
  tables 92
Frame command 83
frames
  creating 82
  inserting text in 94
  selecting 83

G

getting help 25
giving instructions 7
global replacing 47
glossary 37
  entries 37
    changing codes of 40
    creating 37
    deleting 40
    and formatting 39
    inserting 38
    saving 41
    selecting from dialog box 39
  global 41
  vs. Clipboard 37

Glossary command 37, 39–40
Go To button (Help) 27
Grammar command 52
grammar-checking 52
graphics
  as logos 84
  changing size of 84
  cropping 86
  handles 83
  importing 82
  inserting in frames 83
  previewing 84
  Word 82
gridlines, turning on 104
Gridlines command 104

H

handles, graphics 83
header, data document 135
header window 110
Header/Footer command 109–110
headers 108
  adjusting position of 114
  different first-page 109
  viewing 113
heading styles 31, 69
headings
  changing to text 34
  deleting from outline 35
  entering in Outline view 31
  rearranging 36
help
  context-sensitive 27
  getting 25
Help Index command 16, 26, 131
Help Keyboard command 16
Help program 26
Help screen 26–27
hidden text, and printing 91
hyphenating documents 79
Hyphenation command 79

I

icons
  minus 31
  plus 32, 36
  Word for Windows 2
importing
  charts 94
  graphics 82
  spreadsheets 98
indenting tables 90
indents, adjusting 78
information, summary 17
inheriting styles 76
Insert Merge Field button (Print Merge) 140, 144–145
Insert mode 41
Insert Rows command 91
inserting
  date 111
  glossary entries 38
  graphics in frames 83
  merge fields 140
  page breaks 113
  page numbers 111
  time 111
insertion point, moving 4, 6

installing
  graphics files 82
  templates 119
  Word for Windows 2
Italic button 9, 61

J

joining cells 91
Justify button 11, 73
justifying text 73

K

keyboard
  choosing commands with 12
  shortcuts 16
key conventions 4

L

labels, printing 146
legends, moving 96
letterheads, creating 102
lines
  drawing 62, 112
  in tables 93
  selecting 5
Links command 98
lists, formatting 68
locating files 57, 60
logos 84
  in letterheads 102

M

M button (Print Merge) 139, 144
Macro command 128
macro commands 129
Macro window 129
macros
  automatic 121
  AutoNew 128
  changing 127
MAILLABL template 146
Main dictionary 49
main document 134
Manage Distribution List command 124
margins, adjusting 24, 78, 104
Margins button (Print Preview) 24, 114
Maximize button 3, 21
MEMO2 template 122
memos, creating with template 122
menus 12
Merge Cells command 91
merge fields 134
  conditional 144
  inserting 140
merging
  documents 60, 107
    with print merge 141
  to file 142
  graphic files 82
  to printer 142
minus icon 31
modes
  Extend-Selection 6, 42, 128
  Insert 41
  Overtype 41–42

modifying
    styles 73
    templates 124
        appearance of 125
        function of 127
moving
    columns in tables 89
    in documents 4
    insertion point 4, 6
    in outlines 32
    in tables 88
    text 43
        with drag-and-drop 43

N

naming files 16
New button 19, 77, 87, 107, 136
New command 106–107, 119, 131, 146
New Window command 21
next style, setting 76
nonprinting symbols 8, 15
    finding 46
Normal style 69
    restoring 73
Normal template 41, 105–107, 119
Normal View button 33, 36, 69
NORMAL.DOT 41, 106
    restoring original 106
Numbered List button 68, 78
numbering
    outline levels 35
    paragraphs 35
numbers, decimal-aligning in tables 92

O

One Page button (Print Preview) 24
Open button 18, 60
Open command 125
open spacing 16
opening
    documents 18
        from Find File 60
        existing 42
    Macro window 129
    window panes 21
operators, in print merge 145
Options command 14, 69, 75
organizing outlines 36
outline
    levels 31
        adjusting 32
        numbering 35
    screen 31
Outline command 31, 33
Outline view 30, 33
outlines
    adding text to 33
    changing headings to text 34
    collapsing 35
    expanding 35
    organizing 36
    viewing 34
Overtype mode 41
    turning on and off 42
overtyping 42

P

page breaks, inserting 113
Page Layout command 67, 83, 94
Page Layout view 67, 79
Page Number button 111
page numbers, inserting 111
Page Setup command 23, 78, 104
panes, scrolling 22
paragraph
    formats 7
    marks 15
Paragraph command 7, 72, 78–79, 97, 104–105
paragraphs
    numbering 35
    selecting 6
Paste button 42, 77, 89
Paste Cells command 110
Paste command 13, 42–43
Paste Special command 98
pasting text 42
Picture command 83, 85, 87
plus icon 32, 36
predefined styles 70
preserving previous document 18
press releases
    creating 3
        with template 120
PRESS template 120
previewing
    documents 24
    graphics 84
Print button 24, 108
Print button (Print Preview) 24
Print command 25, 27
print merge 134
    comparing expressions in 145
    conditional decisions in 143
    controlling 143
    data documents 134
    header 135
    main documents 134
    operators 145
    uses for 135
Print Merge bar 139, 141
Print Merge button (Print Merge) 142, 148
Print Merge command 136, 138
print merging documents 141
Print Preview 24
Print Preview command 24, 65, 67, 113
print settings, specifying 23
Print Setup command 23, 78
printers, selecting 23
printing
    and hidden text 91
    conditionally 143
    documents 22
    labels 146
    specifying number of copies 25
Promote button (Outline) 32, 34

Q

quitting Word 27

R

rearranging tables 89
records 135
    entering 139
repeating
    commands 75
    Find command 45, 47
Replace command 47, 75
replacing
    styles 75
    text 47
    without confirmation 47
restoring
    original NORMAL.DOT 106
    templates 119
revising documents 41
Ribbon 7
    displaying 2
    and formats 10
    turning on and off 13
Ribbon command 2, 13
Right Align button 11
Row Height command 91
rows
    changing height of 91
    deleting 90
    inserting in tables 91
Ruler 12
    displaying 2
    moving column markers on 90
    scale symbol 12
    turning on and off 14
Ruler command 2, 14

S

Save As command 16, 18, 60, 106, 127
Save button 16, 18, 33, 61, 87, 94, 105, 108, 136
saving
    but preserving previous version 18
    existing documents 18
    glossary entries 41
    new documents 16
    templates 106, 115, 127
    with different name 18
scales
    ruler 12
    table 92
screens
    Help 26–27
    outline 31
scroll bars 5, 20
scrolling 5
    panes 22
Search button (Help) 26
search direction, changing 46
searching for text 44
section breaks 67
sections 65
Select Table command 90, 93–94, 109
selecting
    documents 6, 16
    footers 112
    frames 83
    glossary entries 39
    lines 5
    paragraphs 6

Index

printers 23
sentences 6
tables 93
text 5
words 5–6
selection
   bar 5
   extending 6
sentences, selecting 6
Series In Columns command (Chart) 95
setting up tables 87
Setup program 119
shading 63, 126
shadowed border 126
Show 1 button (Outline) 35
Show 2 button (Outline) 35
Show All button (Outline) 35
size, changing 8–9, 61
Size box 8, 73
small caps 62
spacing
   closed 16
   open 16
specifying
   file search criteria 58
   print settings 23
spell-checking 49
   entire document 49
   selection 51
spelling, correcting 50
Spelling command 49–51
split bar 21
splitting windows 21
spreadsheets
   importing 98
   supported formats 98
starting Word for Windows 2
statistics about files 17
status bar 6, 25
   turning on and off 15
stopping find and replace 47
style area, displaying 69, 75
Style box 56, 69, 71, 77
Style command 73, 76
styles 56, 69
   adding to template 73
   applying 70, 74
      as you type 75
      from keyboard 73
   changing 73
   creating custom 71
   default 70
   defining 72
   finding 75
   heading 31
   Normal 81
   predefined 70
   setting next 76
   transferring 77
   viewing 69
summary information 17
   changing 18, 60

switching directories 19
symbols, nonprinting 8

T

tab-delimited fields 135
Table button 90, 94, 103
table scale 92
tables
   changing
      column width 89
      gridlines 93
      row height 91
   clearing contents of 90
   converting to text 94
   creating 87
   decimal alignment in 92
   drawing lines in 93
   formatting 92
   indenting 90
   inserting rows in 91
   joining cells in 91
   and letterheads 103
   making entries in 88
   moving around 88
   rearranging 89
   selecting 93
   setting up 87
   turning on gridlines 104
Tables button 87
telling Word what to do 7
templates 102, 118
   adding styles to 73
   creating 105
   DATAFILE 139
   installing 119
   MAILLABL 146
   MEMO2 122
   modifying 124
   modifying appearance of 125
   modifying function of 127
   Normal 41
   PRESS 120
   restoring 119
   saving 127
   using 107
   viewing list of 119
text
   adding to outlines 33
   centering 11, 73
   converting to table 94
   copying 42
   deleting 43
   entering in tables 88
   finding 44
   hidden 91
   inserting in frames 94
   justifying 11, 73
   moving 43
   pasting 42
   putting beside table 94
   replacing 47
   right-aligning 11
   searching for 44

selecting 5
time, inserting 111
title bar 18
Toolbar 2, 7, 13
Toolbar command 2, 13
turning on and off
   Extend-Selection mode 7, 42, 128
   field codes 112, 126, 140
   nonprinting symbols 15
   Overtype mode 42
   Ribbon 13
   Ruler 14
   scroll bars 5
   status bar 15
   style area 69, 75
   table gridlines 104
   Toolbar 13
Two Pages button (Print Preview) 24, 113

U

Underline button 61
Undo button 44
undoing editing 44

V

viewing
   headers and footers 113
   list of templates 119
   outlines 34
   styles 69

W

wildcards, using in search 46
windows
   arranging 20
   closing panes 22
   expanding 3
   footer 110
   Footnotes 64
   header 110
   Macro 129
   moving among 20
   splitting 21
WINWORD.INI 14
WMF extension 82
Word for Windows
   icon 2
   installing 2
   quitting 27
   starting 2
Word options, installing 119
WordArt 104
WordBASIC 118, 129
words
   finding whole 46
   selecting 5–6
wordwrap 4
working with windows 20
WYSIWYG 13

Z

Zoom command, 126

Acknowledgments

Thanks to *Garbage* magazine for allowing us to use the data in Chapter 4.

About Online Press

Founded in 1986, Online Press is a group of publishing professionals working to make the presentation and access of information manageable, efficient, accurate, and economical. In 1991, we began publishing our popular *Quick Course* computer-book series, offering streamlined instruction for today's busy professional. At Online Press, it is our goal to help computer users quickly learn what they need to know about today's most popular software programs to get their work done efficiently.

Cover design and photography by Tom Draper Design
Interior text design by Salley Oberlin, Joyce Cox, and Kjell Swedin
Graphics by Steve Lambert and Patrick Kervran
Proofreading by Polly Fox Urban and Christina Smith
Layout by Joyce Cox and Bill Teel
Printed by Viking Press Inc.

Text composition by Online Press in Times Roman, with display type in Helvetica Narrow Bold, using Ventura Publisher and the Linotronic 300 laser imagesetter.

Other *Quick Course* Books

Don't miss the other titles in our *Quick Course* series! Quality books at the unbeatable price of $12.95.

A Quick Course in Windows 3.1
A Quick Course in Excel 4 for Windows
A Quick Course in WordPerfect for Windows
A Quick Course in DOS 5
A Quick Course in WordPerfect 5.1
A Quick Course in Lotus 1-2-3 for Windows
A Quick Course in Quattro Pro for Windows
A Quick Course in Paradox for Windows
A Quick Course in PageMaker for Windows

Plus more to come...

For our latest catalog, call (206) 641-3434 or write to us at:
Online Press Inc., 14320 NE 21st Street, Suite 18, Bellevue, WA 98007